DATE DUE

AP 10'02		
NO 12'02		
FE 2'04		

FOLLETT

The Survivors

Books in the Holocaust Library

The Death Camps
The Final Solution
The Nazis
Nazi War Criminals
The Resistance
The Righteous Gentiles
The Survivors

THE HOLOCAUST LIBRARY

The Survivors

by

ELEANOR H. AYER

Lucent Books, P.O. Box 289011, San Diego, CA 92198-9011

Library of Congress Cataloging-in-Publication Data

Ayer, Eleanor H.
  The survivors / by Eleanor H. Ayer.
    p. cm. — (The Holocaust library)
  Includes bibliographical references and index.
  Summary: Describes the conditions of Holocaust survivors when they were liberated as well as their struggle as they attempt to rebuild their lives.
  ISBN 1-56006-096-4 (alk. paper)
  1. Holocaust survivors—Juvenile literature. 2. Refugees, Jewish—Juvenile literature. 3. Jews—History—1945- —Juvenile literature.
  [1. Holocaust survivors. 2. Refugees. 3. Jews—History—1945-]
  I. Title. II. Series: Holocaust library (San Diego, Calif.)
DS134.A94   1998
940.53'18—dc21
                                          97-27260
                                              CIP
                                               AC

Table of Contents

Foreword

More than eleven million innocent people, mostly Jews but also millions of others deemed "subhuman" by Adolf Hitler such as Gypsies, Russians, and Poles, were murdered by the Germans during World War II. The magnitude and unique horror of the Holocaust continues to make it a focal point in history—not only the history of modern times, but also the entire record of humankind. While the war itself temporarily changed the political landscape, the Holocaust forever changed the way we look at ourselves.

Starting with the European Renaissance in the 1400s, continuing through the Enlightenment of the 1700s, and extending to the Liberalism of the 1800s, philosophers and others developed the idea that people's intellect and reason allowed them to rise above their animal natures and conquer poverty, brutality, warfare, and all manner of evils. Given the will to do so, there was no height to which humanity might not rise. Was not mankind, these people argued, the noblest creation of God—in the words of the Bible, "a little lower than the angels"?

Western Europeans believed so heartily in these concepts that when rumors of mass murders by the Nazis began to emerge, people refused to accept—despite mounting evidence—that such things could take place. Even the Jews who were being deported to the death camps had a hard time believing that they were headed toward extermination. Rational beings, they argued, could not commit such actions. When the veil of secrecy was finally ripped from the death camps, however, the world recoiled in shock and horror. If humanity was capable of such depravity, what was its true nature? Were humans lower even than animals instead of just beneath the angels?

The perpetration of the Holocaust, so far outside the bounds of society's experience, cried out for explanations. For more than a half century, people have sought them. Thousands of books, diaries, sermons, poems, plays, films, and lectures have been devoted to almost every imaginable aspect of the Holocaust, yet it remains one of the most difficult episodes in history to understand.

Some scholars have explained the Holocaust as a uniquely German event, pointing to the racial supremacy theories of German philosophers, the rigidity of German society, and the tradition of obedience to authority. Others have seen it as a uniquely Jewish phenomenon, the culmination of centuries of anti-Semitism in Christian Europe. Still others have said that the Holocaust was a unique combination of these two factors—a set of circumstances unlikely ever to recur.

Such explanations are comfortable and simple—too simple. The Holocaust was neither a German event nor a Jewish event. It was a human event. The same forces—racism, prejudice, fanaticism—that sent millions to the gas chambers have not disappeared. If anything, they have become more evident. One cannot say, "It can't happen again." On a different scale, it has happened again. More than a million Cambodians were killed between 1974 and 1979 by a Communist government. In 1994 thousands of innocent civilians were murdered in tribal warfare between the Hutu and Tutsi tribes in the African nations of Burundi and Rwanda. Christian Serbs in Bosnia embarked on a program of "ethnic cleansing" in the mid-1990s, seeking to rid the country of Muslims.

The complete answer to the Holocaust has proved elusive. Indeed, it may never be found. The search, however, must continue. As author Elie Wiesel, a survivor of the death camps, wrote, "No one has the right to speak for the dead. . . . Still, the story had to be told. In spite of all risks, all possible misunderstandings. It needed to be told for the sake of our children."

Each book in Lucent Books' seven volume Holocaust Library covers a different topic that reveals the full gamut of human response to the Holocaust. *The Nazis*, *The Final Solution*, *The Death Camps*, and *Nazi War Criminals* focus on the perpetrators of the Holocaust and their plan to eliminate the Jewish people. Volumes on *The Righteous Gentiles*, *The Resistance*, and *The Survivors* reveal that humans are capable of being "the noblest creation of God," able to commit acts of bravery and altruism even in the most terrible circumstances.

History offers a way to interpret and reinterpret the past and an opportunity to alter the future. Lucent Books' topic-centered approach is an ideal introduction for students to study such phenomena as the Holocaust. After all, only by becoming knowledgeable about such atrocities can humanity hope to prevent future crimes from occurring. Although such historical lessons seem clear and unavoidable, as historian Yehuda Bauer wrote, "People seldom learn from history. Can we be an exception?"

Chronology of Events

1944

July 23 Majdanek near Lublin, Poland, becomes the first Nazi death camp to be liberated.

1945

January–May Most Nazi death and concentration camps liberated.

May 7 Unconditional surrender of Germany ends World War II in Europe.

August U.S. General Patton grudgingly accompanies General Eisenhower on a tour of the Feldafing Displaced Persons camp in Germany. In August 31 letter to wife he comments that "Actually the Germans are the only decent people left in Europe."

October David Ben-Gurion visits the Displaced Persons camps in Europe and tells survivors that all who want to go to Palestine will be brought there as soon as possible.

December 22 President Truman's order grants special permission to displaced persons who want to enter the United States; some 22,950 arrive.

1946

March 19 Chaim Hirschmann, one of two survivors of the Belzec death camp, is killed upon his return to Lublin, Poland.

July 4 Pogrom in Kielce, Poland, against 150 returning Jewish survivors leaves forty-two dead and fifty wounded.

July 22 Agents of the radical Jewish group *Irgun* blow up the King David Hotel in Jerusalem, killing ninety-one British, Arabs, and Jews.

1947

One million displaced persons remain in the camps of Europe.

July 18 Jewish refugee ship *Exodus* is rammed by British destroyers off the coast of Haifa, Palestine. Passengers and crew are arrested and returned to Europe.

November 29 United Nations General Assembly adopts a resolution for partitioning Palestine into two states, an Arab and a Jewish. The partition becomes effective in May 1948, when the British mandate in Palestine expires.

1948

April 9 Jewish extremist groups massacre the Arab village of Deir Yassin.

May 14 British Mandate to rule Palestine expires. David Ben-Gurion declares birth of the Jewish State of Israel. Fighting between the Arabs and Jews—the Israeli War of Independence—begins.

May 28 Arabs overtake the Old City of Jerusalem in the Israeli War of Independence.

June 11 First UN-supervised truce in the War of Independence begins. It is broken on July 9 in a fight for the Negev. Second truce takes effect July 18.

June 25 Immigration law passed, allowing 200,000 immigrants to enter the United States over the next two years, but with stiff restrictions. Ultimately the law is modified to be less discriminatory against Jews.

June 26 Allied pilots begin largest airlift in world history, flying tons of food, fuel, supplies into communist-controlled Berlin to relieve the Soviet blockade against the city.

September 17 Count Folke Bernadotte, UN mediator in the Arab-Israeli war, and his assistant, are assassinated by a Jewish terrorist group.

October 14 Third round of the Israeli War of Independence begins with Egyptians fighting the Israelis in the Negev.

1949

January 12 Peace talks begin between Arabs and Israelis. Eventually armistices are signed between Israel and individual Arab countries.

February David Ben-Gurion elected the first prime minister of Israel.

August 14 Body of Theodor Herzl, father of Zionism, arrives in Israel and is buried on a hill above Jerusalem.

1950

Law of Return passed by the Knesset, the Israeli Parliament, grants every Jew worldwide the right to settle permanently in Israel.

December 17 Central Committee of the Jewish Displaced Persons is disbanded. All refugees who wanted to immigrate to Israel have arrived.

1954

Law passed by the Knesset grants citizenship to any Jewish immigrant.

The Handful Who Survived

Oftentimes people who have witnessed the worst aspects of human existence emerge with a greater capacity to laugh, love, and appreciate life more fully than those who have not experienced such extremes. This can be said of many survivors of the *Shoah*, or Holocaust—the Jewish genocide that occurred at the hands of the Nazis during World War II. In percentages far higher than an average cross-section of society, Holocaust survivors have educated themselves, become respected professionals in their fields, and achieved financial success in the decades since World War II.

It hasn't been easy. Even as they were liberated from Nazi death and concentration camps in 1945, they found themselves fighting the same demons that spawned the Holocaust: prejudice, anti-Semitism, lack of concern for fellow human beings. The lessons of hatred that the Holocaust should have taught had not been learned. In the postwar world, survivors were once again shunned, rejected, persecuted, and denied a normal existence. And while they were battling this new rejection, they had also to battle the demons of memory—the ghosts of relatives who had not come back, a fear of authority figures, the guilt of having lived when so many others died.

To rebuild their lives, the *She'erit Haple-*

tah, the "handful who survived," relied on the same qualities that had helped them stay alive while six million of their fellow Jews perished. They were adaptable, they maintained a sense of humor, they helped each other, they kept a low profile in society. Above all, they maintained a sense of self-respect and decency.

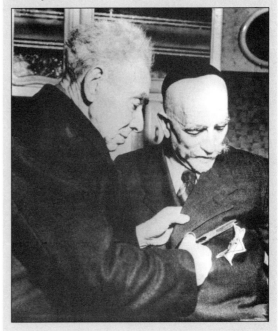

Two survivors from the Netherlands celebrate the end of World War II by cutting off the yellow Star of David that marked them as "Jood."

The strong individuals who survived the hell of Adolf Hitler's Final Solution must stand as an inspiration to subsequent generations. There is much to learn from Holocaust survivors, who have endured the worst of life and worked their way back to the top. There is the lesson of hope in the face of overwhelming defeat and depression. There is the lesson taught by teenage diarist Anne Frank, who said that despite everything, she still believed that people were basically good.

Some survivors feel that they have a responsibility to hate the Nazi perpetrators, bystanders, and even the German people, as a sort of memorial to loved ones who perished. Auschwitz survivor Helen Waterford disagrees. Hatred, she says, is a boomerang that only destroys the sender.

> While we will forever mourn, revenge must never detract from remembering our dead. To condemn *all* Germans reduces us to the level of the Nazis, who hated every Jew, every gypsy, every Slav. . . . If we follow the scripture "an eye for an eye . . ." we all will eventually be blind.[1]

The State of Survivors at Liberation

The living dead were more awful. They could still open their eyes, but they did not see. They had ears but could scarcely hear. Their wrecked bodies and tortured minds had reduced them to a level below animals. They were helpless skeletons; hollow frames with departed souls. The dead were more fortunate than these live corpses. They still breathed, but they did not live.[2]
—Congressman Dewey Short, who visited Buchenwald, Nordhausen, and Dachau shortly after liberation

What met the liberating armies as they entered the death and concentration camps of Central and Eastern Europe in 1944–1945 was a scene of universal, unbelievable horror. Worse, even, than the piles of unburied bodies and the overpowering stench of death was the condition of inmates who had survived. Their bodies were emaciated due to starvation and disease, so ravaged that they had lost 50 to 60 percent of their body weight and inches off their height. Most survivors weighed no more than sixty to eighty pounds.

Hoping to escape punishment, Nazi leaders had made a last-minute, frantic effort to cover up the evidence of mass murder at the death camps. They had burned buildings, destroyed the crematoria where bodies had been burned, and sent those who could still walk on death marches to camps nearer Germany. In most cases, however, their efforts came too late to hide the evidence. Those prisoners who survived made it their mission to describe in detail the brutality and inhumane treatment of the millions who had died.

A Shocking Tour of the Camps

Majdanek, a death camp near Lublin, Poland, was the first to be liberated on July 23, 1944. "I have never seen a more abominable sight," wrote one Soviet journalist. Here, where 600,000 to 1,000,000 human beings were murdered during the camp's existence, the Red Army found "1,000 living corpses"[3] on liberation day.

General Dwight D. Eisenhower, who had led the Allies' successful invasion of Europe, was one of the generals who liberated the Buchenwald concentration camp in central Germany. Among the survivors was Elie Wiesel, who became a major spokesman on the Holocaust and later received the Nobel Peace Prize. A seasoned general, Eisenhower had seen the horror, cruelty, and sorrow of war. But of Buchenwald, he later admitted, "I have never felt able to describe my emotional reaction when I

Shortly after liberation prisoners in various stages of starvation pose for the camera at a concentration camp in Ebensee, Austria.

came face to face with indisputable evidence of Nazi brutality and ruthless disregard for every shred of human decency. . . . I am certain, however, that I have never at any time experienced an equal sense of shock."[4]

Farther north in Germany was Bergen-Belsen, the concentration camp where Anne Frank, teenage author of the famous diary, died of typhus. The typhus epidemic had killed thousands of prisoners, and their bodies had been left to rot in the sun. Of the 60,000 people still alive at liberation, 14,000 died of starvation, typhus, and other diseases within a few days.

At Dachau, a camp near Munich, 33,000 prisoners remained alive when Allied armies liberated it in late April 1945. Dachau, in operation since March 1933, housed what one American general called "a very high class bunch of people. . . . There were professors, doctors, lawyers, engineers, politicians, priests, and ministers."[5] One of the best-known survivors was Pastor Martin Niemöller, who had tried to turn Lutherans against Adolf Hitler and come to the defense of Jews.

Near Hitler's boyhood home of Linz, Austria, was Mauthausen, the infamous concentration camp where prisoners slaved in stone quarries. The work was brutal; 1¹/₂ to 2 million people perished in Mauthausen and its sub- or satellite camps. When American troops liberated it on May 4, 1945, they found 5,419 survivors. Altogether, 38,906 Jews had perished there—approximately one-third of all prisoners. Hardened criminals and political prisoners made up the majority of victims. "Priority was given to the plight of the deathly sick and starving,"[6]

writes historian Abram Sachar. Those who could travel were urged to head home, and by the end of May only a few—those who had no place to go—remained in the camp.

Survivors of the "Model Ghetto"

Theresienstadt in Czechoslovakia, the Nazis' "model ghetto" that became a concentration camp, was liberated on May 8, 1945, by Soviet soldiers. The scene there was similar to that at other camps: 17,320

(Below) These corpses at Belsen, Germany, lie in mute and terrible testimony to the millions of Jews who did not survive the concentration camps. (Right) General Dwight D. Eisenhower watches while former prisoners show how they were tortured by Nazi guards.

Survivors at Theresienstadt concentration camp welcome the Soviet army during liberation on May 9, 1945.

people still alive, but many of them close to death. Hunger overpowered the survivors, wrote one soldier: "In their animal wildness, mad with starvation, they are dangerous. It is impossible to mete food out to them in the usual way; they immediately attack each other, choking and beating one another for every scrap."[7]

One of the most famous survivors of Theresienstadt was Rabbi Leo Baeck, a former leader of the Jewish community in Berlin. Baeck survived the psychological horror of the camps by reading the works of great philosophers and religious leaders. On liberation day, he watched in amazement as Nazi commandant Karl Rahm left the camp. Not one of the hundreds of prisoners around him sought revenge. "Look at it," he remarked with pride. "This can happen only with Jews. Of all the people here, not one person lifted a stone to throw at him. They could have strangled him if they wanted."[8]

The Handful Who Survived

The *She'erit Hapletah*—in Hebrew "Surviving Remnant"—were the European Jews who survived Hitler's Final Solution. Two-thirds of the nine million prewar European

Jews were dead. Approximately 90 percent of the dead were Ashkenazim—the Yiddish-speaking Jews of Poland, Lithuania, Latvia, and Czechoslovakia. The Sephardim, the other large division of Jewry who descended from the Jews of Spain and Portugal, were not killed in such large numbers.

Among the *She'erit Hapletah*, approximately 300,000 were survivors of ghettos, concentration camps, and death marches. The rest had managed to escape or hide, avoiding capture by the Gestapo. One of those was Samuel Pisar, who, with a group of teenage boys, survived the last days of the war in a hayloft in the Bavarian section of Germany. Peeking through the wooden slats in the barn walls, he watched as a huge tank approached their hiding place:

> In an instant, the realization flooded me; I was looking at the insignia of the United States army. . . . My skull seemed to burst. With a wild roar, I broke through the thatched roof, leaped to the ground, and ran toward the tank. . . . Recalling the only English I knew . . . I yelled at the top of my lungs, "God bless America!". . . In a few minutes, all of us were free.[9]

The Joy and Sorrow of Liberation

Liberation day, for those who were mentally and physically able, was a day of wildly mixed emotions. Many were so overcome with hunger that their only thought was to find food. "Our first act as free men," writes Buchenwald survivor Elie Wiesel, "was to throw ourselves onto the provisions. We thought only of that. Not of revenge, not of our families. Nothing but bread."[10]

Most could not comprehend that after years of torture they were at last free. Some felt little joy in their freedom because of the tremendous losses they had suffered. Others, like Auschwitz survivor Helen Waterford, were overcome with a new love for life:

> The lilies of the valley were never more beautiful than in May of 1945. . . . I walked out the gate at the Women's Labor Camp in Kratzau, Czechoslovakia—FREE! I threw myself into the large field of these dainty little flowers, embracing as many as I could, overwhelmed by their fragrance, which filled me with joy, hope, rebirth and a new security.[11]

Not all survivors shared Helen's optimism. Liberation meant that they must now come face-to-face with the tragedy of the Holocaust. The search for missing relatives could begin, but it might well end in the discovery of death or, worse yet, with no news at all—ever. Hadassah Bimko, a survivor of Bergen-Belsen, was among the joyless:

> For the great part of the liberated Jews . . . there was no ecstasy, no joy at our liberation. We had lost our families, our homes. We had no place to go, nobody to hug, nobody who was waiting for us, anywhere. We had been liberated from . . . the fear of death, but we were not free from the fear of life.[12]

Coming to Grips with Freedom

After months or years of living hour by hour and day by day, many survivors felt sheer surprise at being liberated. Freedom was incomprehensible. Writes Italian survivor Primo Levi, "We had to make an effort to convince ourselves of [freedom] and no one had time to enjoy the thought. All around us lay destruction and death."[13]

Because they had lived so close to death

(Above) An inmate is overcome with grief after learning that he is not leaving with the first group to go to the hospital after liberation. (Left) Perhaps the saddest fate was shared by people like this man who were able to survive until liberation but were too far gone with starvation to live beyond it.

for so long, some survivors felt more dead than alive. "Everyone lay motionless," recalls survivor Sonia Rosenfeld of her liberation by Soviet soldiers. "No one could utter a word. It is impossible to be freed when one already has one leg underground."[14]

Others would not allow themselves to believe they were really free. So many times authorities had lied to them that they saw no reason to be hopeful now. "We, the cowed and emaciated inmates of the camp, did not believe we were free," recalls Bergen-Belsen survivor Josef Rosensaft. "It seemed to us a dream which would soon turn again into cruel reality."[15]

Disbelief, fatigue, starvation, disease, anger—the liberators came to expect these reactions among survivors. What they found hard to comprehend was apathy. After years of torture, the prisoners were finally free and able to leave, but many did nothing. They simply sat and stared. They made no move toward freedom. Bela Braver, an Auschwitz survivor who was liberated from a Czech work camp, explains, "We did not laugh, we were not happy, we were apathetic." When the liberating Russian general came in, "he told us that he was delighted, as this was the first camp in which he had found people still alive. He started to cry; but we didn't. He wept and we didn't." [16]

Viktor Frankl, a psychiatrist and survivor from Vienna, Austria, explains this reaction among survivors: "We did not yet belong to this world. . . . 'Freedom'—we repeated to ourselves, and yet we could not grasp it." Writes Holocaust historian Michael Berenbaum, "Only later—and for some it was much later or never—was liberation actually liberating." [17]

"Canned-Goods Victims"

It was hard, at first, for many survivors to realize that they were even alive. "We unlearned to laugh, we cannot cry any more, we do not understand our freedom yet," Zalman Grinberg told his fellow survivors in 1945. "All this because we are still with

Survivors of Auschwitz concentration camp in Poland stare out from behind barbed wire at their liberators. Having witnessed so many horrible events, some survivors greeted liberation with mixed emotions, many feeling strong guilt for having survived an ordeal that killed so many.

Elie Wiesel: Survivor of Vision

When the Buchenwald concentration camp was liberated in May 1945, Elie Wiesel was sixteen years old. His parents and his sister had died in the camps, and Elie was barely alive. From his recovery bed in a hospital, he struggled to a mirror to look at himself, something he had not done for years. "From the depths of the mirror," writes Wiesel in *Night*, "a corpse gazed back at me. The look in his eyes, as they stared into mine, has never left me."

After the war, Wiesel did not return to his native Hungary but went instead to France, where he learned French and worked for ten years as a journalist. From France he moved to Israel and eventually to the United States, where he became a professor at Boston University.

Night, an autobiographical account of Wiesel's life in Buchenwald, was the first of more than twenty books that he wrote about the Holocaust. His writings have earned him the title "bard of the Holocaust." He writes, says one admirer, "out of infinite pain, partly to honor the dead, but also to warn the living—to warn [them] that it could happen again and that it must never happen again."

Wiesel's determination, not only to survive but to sound a warning against future Holocausts, led him to lecture and teach, conduct workshops, and become a sought-after Holocaust expert. His writings have won French and American literary awards, and in 1985 he received the Nobel Peace Prize. Yet in his books, Wiesel does not always develop themes of harmony and peace. "Every Jew, somewhere in his being," he writes in *Legends of Our Time*, "should set apart a zone of hate—healthy, virile hate—for what the German personifies and for what persists in the German. To do otherwise would be a betrayal of the dead."

Elie Wiesel, survivor of Buchenwald, was a young man of sixteen at the time of liberation.

our dead comrades. . . . We are not alive. We are dead!"[18] A British nurse, helping to care for a group of male survivors, had the same report. "Their dead eyes rarely kindled a response," she later wrote. "[These men] seemed to have forgotten that they ever had wives or children. They only cared for the food trolley. Every other instinct or emotion had been suppressed except the will to survive."[19]

But often, when food was offered by the liberators, the survivors' digestive systems could not tolerate it. Deprived of food, they had stayed alive on stored fat and muscle fiber in their bodies, and so their digestive systems had begun to cease functioning. Children could not drink whole milk; it was too rich. Adults had trouble digesting simple foods like butter. Those who did succumb to temptation often found themselves vomiting or with severe stomach cramps and diarrhea. Portions had to be small because the victims' stomachs had shrunk so much.

Survivors had adapted to the lack of calories and nutrition by learning to move slowly, to conserve every ounce of strength. They marveled as their liberators, well fed and healthy, moved about the camps in a

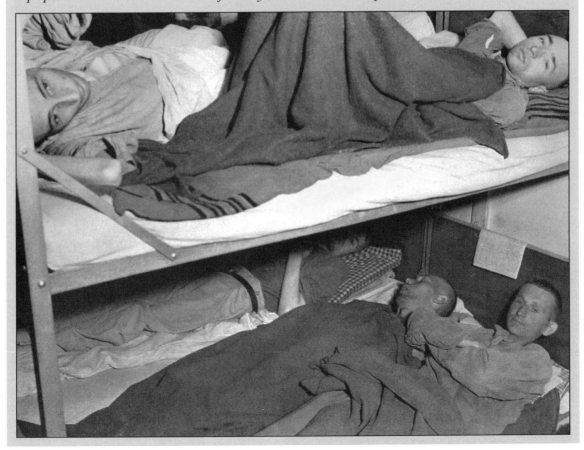

After being liberated from Dachau, survivors must sleep two to a bunk at an Allied hospital. Allies were unprepared to deal with the thousands of deathly ill concentration camp survivors.

hurry. "These men seemed not to know that one could live in slow motion, that energy was something you saved,"[20] recalls Fania Fenelon, a Bergen-Belsen survivor.

The liberators moved quickly because they saw the urgency of getting immediate help if these victims were to survive. "One has to take a tour round and see their faces," wrote one British officer to his wife in a letter from Bergen-Belsen, "their slow staggering gait and feeble movements. The state of their minds is plainly written on their faces, as starvation has reduced their bodies to skeletons."[21]

In those first days of liberation, writes historian Abram Sachar, "it [was] difficult to distinguish between the living, the barely living, and . . . the dead. [The liberators'] most dedicated efforts to salvage the human wreckage could not save tens of thousands who died in the first weeks after freedom."[22] The toll of Jews, as closely as it could be tallied under such chaotic conditions, was twenty-seven thousand who died in the camps *after* liberation.

Many of those would have died anyway; their weight had dropped beyond a point that would sustain life. Others might have lived, but when put in the presence of food,

Female survivors are evacuated from Bergen-Belsen on April 28, 1945.

Jewish War Orphans of Holland

On July 14, 1942, the Nazis, who had invaded Holland two years earlier, began rounding up Dutch Jews, supposedly for slave labor in Germany. In reality the Jews, including children, were to be deported to death or concentration camps. Well-meaning Gentiles (non-Jews) with connections in the underground movement hurriedly did their own roundup of Jewish children to save them from deportation. They placed these youngsters in Gentile homes, where they were kept hidden.

In all, 4,138, children went into hiding during this action (*Aktion* in German). But at the end of the war, three years later, only about half of the children could find their parents. The remaining 2,041 were orphans, whose fate was to be decided by the War Orphans Committee.

There was one major problem, however. Most of the orphaned Jewish children had been living with Christians and were being raised in the Christian faith. According to Dutch law, children were to be educated according to the religious beliefs of their parents. In ordinary times, this would mean that the orphans should be raised in Jewish households. But these were not ordinary times.

The War Orphans Committee believed that the children should be left in their foster homes, rather than disrupt what little security they had. But Jewish organizations and some relatives of the orphans, who themselves could not take in additional family members, thought the children should be placed with Jewish families. The debate caused great argument in Holland for years after the war. In the end, however, fewer than 20 percent of the orphans ended up in Jewish homes. Very few of them ever returned to the Jewish faith.

---

ate more than their digestive systems and vital organs could tolerate. "We called them canned-goods victims,"[23] explains one survivor, because the food that the liberating armies brought in was mostly in tin cans. Others "died from sheer joy," recalls a witness on the scene. "They had lived on hope, on fear and on their sheer nerves for so long that the sudden relaxation, when it came, was too much for them."[24]

What Qualities Motivated Survivors to Live?

What tactics or traits in their personalities helped some prisoners live while others died?

Most survivors agreed that it was important to keep thinking of themselves as human beings, not as numbers or laborers in uniforms, which was what the Nazis wanted. Psychiatrist Viktor Frankl, a prisoner in Theresienstadt and Auschwitz, survived by going into a fantasy world when the real one became too unbearable. Frankl was able to block out the horror around him and fill his mind with memories of pleasant times past. "By this method," he later wrote, "I succeeded somehow in rising above the situation, above the suffering of the moment, and I observed them [the death camp ordeals] as if they were already of the past."[25]

Others, particularly non-Jewish survivors, lived only to seek revenge against the Nazis. One was Alexander (Sasha) Pechersky, a Soviet army officer and prisoner who had organized the escape from the Sobibor death camp. "We are not allowed to give up on life," Pechersky told his fellow prisoners. "We must live in order to take our revenge. . . . No one can do our work for us."[26] Pecherky got his revenge. Twenty years after the war ended, he was a major witness for the prosecution in the trial of twelve Nazis, ten of whom were found guilty and hanged.

Psychiatrist Bruno Bettelheim, also a survivor, believed that people who were very religious or had strong political beliefs stood the best chances of survival. Others said it had more to do with ruthlessness, that certain individuals did whatever was necessary—lied, stole, or killed, without regard for their fellow human beings—in order to survive. Time was a factor, too. Prisoners who were not captured by the Gestapo until late in the war had a better chance of enduring the rigors of the camps because they were not there as long.

But perhaps, suggests literary critic Terrence Des Pres, quoting a death camp survivor, the qualities for survival are not so easily defined. "It wasn't the ruthlessness that enabled an individual to survive. It was an intangible quality . . . an overriding thirst—perhaps, too, a talent for life, and a faith in life."[27]

2 The Reawakening

For the survivor, coming back to life after being so close to death was a joyous and yet a terrible ordeal. Survivors' worlds had changed forever; nothing would be the same again. "The moment of liberation was hopeful yet fearful,"[28] writes historian Michael Berenbaum. They had lived in a world of lies and deceit for so long that they trusted no one and were suspicious of everyone. Nightmares were common, writes Abram Sachar, and memories would not disappear:

> There was a cold sweat at the sight of a physician or a nurse in a white coat. There was panic if a child were absent for more than a few moments. There was dread when one sat or stood with back to a door or window. There was erosion of trust even of one another.[29]

Even though they were fed and cared for, survivors instinctively hoarded bread and other items useful to survival. A British nurse, working in a military hospital, recalls, "[We] would find, while making the beds, a slice of corned beef, a potato or a piece of bread hidden under a pillow, for they could not yet be sure that another day would bring more food."[30]

While they were still fighting for physical survival, victims of the *Shoah* (as the Holocaust is called in Hebrew) also had to deal with their ravaged minds. Feelings of guilt were very common: "Why did I survive when all those around me died?" Some had lost all sense of emotion; they could no longer laugh, love, or cry. A rabbi who was helping at liberation recalls pulling a young boy from a pile of corpses and breaking into tears at the pathetic sight. Hoping to cheer the boy, he overcame his horror and began to laugh and joke with the child.

"How old are you," he asked.

"Older than you," the youngster replied.

"How can you say that?" asked the rabbi.

"[Because] you laugh and cry like a little boy," the child replied, "but I haven't laughed for years and I don't even cry any more. So tell me, who is older?"[31]

Loathing Rather than Pity

If compassion, help, and respect were what the survivors deserved, it is far from what they got. "What those who survived did not know when 'liberation' came," writes Abram Sachar, "was that their ordeal was by no means over. They now faced renewed rejection, and it came from the governments and the peoples of the Allied world."[32]

Perhaps the horror was too great to comprehend. Or perhaps people were so tired of war that they wanted nothing to do with survivors and their stories. Maybe the gap between Jewish victims and Gentile, or non-Jew bystanders was simply too great to bridge. Whatever the case, many survivors found little sympathy or understanding in the outside world. Writes historian Paul Johnson:

An act of genocide had been carried out. As the camps were opened and the full extent of the calamity became known, some Jews in their innocence expected an outraged humanity to comprehend the magnitude of the crime and say with one thunderous voice: this is enough. Anti-Semitism must end. We must be done with it once and for all, draw a line under this stupendous outrage, and start history afresh. . . . But that is not how human societies work.[33]

"Even in Europe," writes Johnson, "there was often loathing, rather than pity, for the bewildered survivors." Such a reaction from their fellow human beings, after all they had endured, made many Jewish survivors angry at the non-Jewish world. Sonia Zilka, born in Slovakia in 1937, spent the war in hiding with Jewish partisans—bands of independent fighters who lived in the woods and harassed German soldiers in an effort to disrupt their actions. After liberation, she returned to her prewar home of Michalovce, where she faced a reception like that of many European Jews:

The houses were still there, but [the people] would not accept us. The gentiles really didn't behave nicely, they made us feel that we were unwanted. I remember hearing on the street over and over: "Why didn't they kill you?" They were very upset that we had come back; they didn't want us there.[34]

Dazed and undernourished, these inmates of Lager Nordhausen concentration camp still wear their filthy prison rags as they pose shortly after liberation.

Madeline Deutsch, a teenage survivor of Auschwitz, was one of thousands who immigrated to the United States after liberation. She was delighted, she said, to be "after all these years, free." But at the same time she remained, in her own mind, an outsider: "There was nobody that was Jewish that was my age. And at that point I could not communicate with anybody other than a Jew. I just couldn't! Everybody [else] was the enemy."[35]

Anti-Semitism Continues to Thrive

Thus survivors once again faced the same evil that had bred the Holocaust: anti-Semitism. In the U.S.-occupied sector of Germany, the adviser on Jewish affairs wrote, "only the presence of the American military safeguards the Jewish people." But even American soldiers were not immune to anti-Semitism, as a 1946 poll revealed. Of those surveyed, 22 percent said "the Germans had good reason to distrust the Jews." Ten percent felt that "the Germans were justified in launching the war."[36]

So discouraging was this resurgence of hatred after all they had endured in the Holocaust that some survivors considered suicide. In the KZ (concentration camp), observed one, "we at least had liberation to hope for, to keep us going. Now what was there?"[37]

As it had been during the war, Eastern Europe continued as a hotbed of anti-Semitism. When Theresienstadt was liberated on May 8, 1945, fifteen-year-old Ben Helfgott and his cousin Gershon were among the survivors still clinging to life. Ecstatic to be free, Ben and Gershon headed for their home in Poland. At the border, they were stopped at gunpoint by two Polish police, who threw them up against a wall and shouted filthy, hateful remarks. Although they

Jewish refugee children arrive in New York from Germany. Their final destination is Philadelphia, where they will be placed in foster homes.

stopped short of killing the boys, their anti-Semitic spirit was clear.

One of the worst incidents was a pogrom (massacre) in Kielce, Poland, on July 4, 1946. One hundred fifty Jewish survivors of the town had returned after the war, looking for their homes and families. They were met by a mob of angry Poles, who killed forty-two and wounded fifty.

In Lublin, Poland, Leon Felhendler, a survivor who organized the revolt at the Sobibor death camp on October 14, 1943, was killed in an anti-Semitic attack. In a similar incident on March 19, 1946, Chaim

Liberation did not end Jewish survivors' misery. Anti-Semites continued to attack and kill Jews. Here, mourners gather to grieve for the victims of the Kielce, Poland, pogrom in 1946.

Hirschmann, one of the two survivors of the Belzec death camp, was killed. It was clear to the Jews of Eastern Europe that they were neither safe nor welcome in their old homes.

Coping with the Outside World

Survivors were different; they were misunderstood. They did not fit into a world that wanted only to look to the future, laugh, and be happy. Said Dr. Zalman Grinberg in a speech to survivors late in 1945, "It seems to us that for the time being mankind does not understand what we have gone through and what we have experienced. We fear we will not be understood in [the] future."[38]

Jewish survivors reacted to their heritage in one of two ways. The first was to deny or reject their Jewishness, which often caused problems among families or close friends. Zlata Tauber, born in 1941, did not remember her parents at all. She knew only that she had been in Russia during the war. Later she learned she had a brother living in Poland.

Schindler's Updated List

In 1993 Steven Spielberg's film *Schindler's List* renewed the world's interest in the Holocaust. The film tells the story of German businessman Oskar Schindler, who befriended Nazi officials in order to save the lives of hundreds of Jews. The final scene shows a recent gathering of the *Schindlerjude*—the Jews who were once on Schindler's list—but it doesn't tell what happened to them in the years after the Holocaust. *Miami Herald* journalist Elinor Brecher interviewed dozens of *Schindlerjude* and filled in their stories. In her book *Schindler's Legacy*, she offers testimony from thirty of those survivors. Says Brecher in her introduction:

> The senses remember, even as the intellect struggles to forget. Some survivors can't look at or listen to trains, pass smokestacks, or wait on lines. Others can't tolerate tardiness or the waste of food. They wolf their meals. The sound of spoken German makes some of them physically ill. Dogs terrify a few of them, especially big dogs like Danes, shepherds, and Dalmatians—the breeds favored by the Nazis. Many still jump when the phone rings, their voices prickly with dread when they answer. . . . Irrational fears torment them. One *Schindlerjude* told me about American survivor friends who go to bed every night behind a forest of deadbolts, convinced the Nazis will come in the dark and drag them away.

Not all of Schindler's Jews are haunted by fear and nightmares. Some seem to treasure life now more than ever. "Their . . . lifestyles are equally varied," writes Brecher. "A multi-millionaire New Jersey developer; a Cleveland tailor who works out of his basement; a retired New York cafe violinist; a Baltimore fabric-store owner; a Pittsburgh cantor; a Los Angeles high school shop teacher; a world-famous Manhattan commercial photographer." These survivors' outlooks are as varied as their fates, but they share one common thread: they all owe their survival to Oskar Schindler.

Oskar Schindler (second from right) poses with some of the people he rescued during the Holocaust.

These Jewish survivors leave the anti-Semitism of Poland for a chance at a better life in Czechoslovakia. Polish Jews reported vicious anti-Semitic attacks such as the one in Kielce. One survivor reported that a pamphlet circulated claiming that "Ten Jews will be killed for every Pole executed in the pogrom trials at Kielce."

But, explained a woman who interviewed her, "he [did] not want to be a Jew because of the persecutions they had to go through. She [Zlata] therefore renounced . . . him."[39]

Al Feuerstein did not renounce his Jewish heritage, but he admitted that in the early postwar years he was not comfortable with it. "I was afraid," he remembers, thinking back on his first days in the United States in 1946. "I was afraid to be a Jew. My friends told me, 'Don't worry. We have a constitution. It can never happen again.' I

said, 'Germany was a democracy. It had a constitution too.'"[40]

The other reaction was to embrace Judaism with new zeal. This attitude was often accompanied by a mistrust of the non-Jewish world and a fierce desire to establish a Jewish homeland in Palestine. For nearly two thousand years, Jews had tried unsuccessfully to fit into other cultures: "We had no reason to trust the non-Jewish world, and their behavior . . . even after the extermination by the Nazis, did much to increase this lack of trust in a world which did not save, and could not even find a home for, the remnants of the Holocaust."[41]

Adjusting to the Loss of Family and Friends

Survivors fortunate enough to find their homes and communities still intact began the desperate search for missing friends and family members. Bulletin boards posted "In search of . . ." notices for the missing. It was a crude way to find loved ones, but in the chaos of postwar Europe, with telephone and telegraph lines down and mail service a shambles, bulletin boards were often the best way. The Red Cross kept lists of known survivors, but with millions of people on the move, keeping the lists accurate was nearly impossible. As the weeks went by with no messages of hope, many families had to face the grim truth that their loved ones might never be found.

Loss of family, friends, and community was often harder for the survivors to bear than what they had endured in the concentration camps. The loneliness was overwhelming.

A bulletin board at the World Jewish Congress in London posts notices from survivors attempting to find lost family members.

The Lost Communities

As survivors attempted to find their way home amid the rubble and chaos of postwar Europe, many had to face the fact that their prewar towns no longer existed. During the war, some five thousand Jewish communities or *shtetls* were severely damaged or destroyed by the Germans.

At the United States Holocaust Memorial Museum in Washington, D.C., is the three-story-high Tower of Faces exhibit. On the walls of this tower are thousands of prewar photographs of people who once inhabited the Lithuanian *shtetl* of Eishishok. Yaffa Sonenson Eliach, the woman who collected the photos for the Tower of Faces, was four years old in September 1941, when Hitler's SS executed most of the village's 3,400 Jews. Yaffa was one of only twenty-nine people to survive. Eishishok was only one of thousands of *shtetls* overrun by the Nazis.

The two towers of the museum's main building are connected by a series of glass bridges. Visitors walking across the long fourth-floor bridge can read the names of the more than five thousand towns, etched on the glass, that were severely damaged or destroyed by the Germans. Skopje, Split, Sušak . . . and more, and more, and more.

A similar exhibit can be seen at Yad Vashem, the Holocaust Martyrs' and Heroes' Remembrance Authority in Jerusalem. Called the Valley of the Destroyed Communities, it covers six acres and is filled with tall, rocky structures on which are engraved the names of the five thousand ruined *shtetls*. Throughout the Valley, shaded areas with benches have been set aside for meditation, where visitors can grieve or simply contemplate the enormity of the Holocaust.

A visitor to the Holocaust Memorial Museum looks at a display of photographs that show families in Eishishok, Lithuania, where most of the town's Jews were killed by Nazi death squads.

"After the war, the urge to marry, both as a flight from loneliness and out of a desire to replace the people who had been lost, was very strong," writes researcher Yael Danieli. Such unions she calls "marriages of despair."[42]

According to Jewish custom, a widow cannot remarry unless she can produce witnesses who have seen her husband dead. Because concentration camp survivors rarely could do this, Chief Rabbi Isaac Herzog of Palestine allowed second marriages if a witness could verify that the first spouse had been part of a concentration camp selection or was deported to a death camp.

Survivors often married other survivors, feeling that only someone who had endured the Holocaust could possibly understand their state of mind. One survivor offered this proposal to his prospective bride, "I am alone. I have no one, I have lost everything. You are alone. You have no one. You have lost everything. Let us be alone together."[43]

CHAPTER

3 Millions of Displaced Persons

The roads of Europe were jammed with columns of people trudging on foot, on bicycles, in horse-drawn wagons and in automobiles that in many cases had been stolen. At the same time, freight cars that once had carried troops to war and Jews to slaughter now hauled an army of ". . . compass-point citizens" north, south, east and west across the ravaged face of Europe.[44]

Cities were heaps of rubble. Roads and bridges had been destroyed by the advancing Allies and the retreating Germans. Rail lines had been bombed, making train service spotty at best. During the war, more

Displaced survivors flee Poland after the war. Masses of homeless lined the streets of Europe immediately after liberation.

than fifty million Europeans had been uprooted from their homes. Now, at war's end, survivors were anxious to begin rebuilding their lives. They headed out, often with no clear idea of where they were going. It was the largest and most chaotic migration of human beings in the history of the world.

More than two-thirds of the Europeans displaced by the war had ended up in another region of their own country. For them, returning home was not quite as difficult as it was for the millions who found themselves in foreign lands. Those displaced persons, as the uprooted people were called, included not only deported Jews, but soldiers who had been shipped to foreign fronts, and civilians as well.

Perhaps the most hated group of displaced persons were Germans living outside Germany. Many of these people had been sent to Eastern Europe as part of Hitler's plan to establish lebensraum, "living space." With the collapse of the Third Reich, they became the defeated people. They were treated without mercy, harassed, and thrown out of the places where they were living. In Czechoslovakia, Poland, and other countries overrun by Germany during the war, natives at last took revenge on the hated Germans. Reported one refugee:

> Hundreds of bandits—many of them 12 to 16 years old—sprang like cats onto the train and took away absolutely everything from the voyagers, undressing them to shirt and underwear. Terrible cries of distress were raised as the Poles trampled upon children and old people in their lust to loot.[45]

What to Do with the Human Remnants of War

Because of the chaos in Europe at war's end, it was impossible to tell just how many displaced persons were on the road. A researcher at the United States Holocaust Memorial Museum says, "Seven to nine million displaced people [were] living in countries not their own. [Some] six million returned to their native lands. But more than one million refused."[46]

Many of those who refused were Jews who did not want to return to an anti-Semitic homeland, or Eastern Europeans fleeing communism. At war's end, Joseph Stalin, the Soviet Union's harsh dictator, set up communist governments in Poland, East Germany, the Baltic countries, Ukraine, Yugoslavia, and other areas that had come under Soviet control.

Russian soldiers found themselves in a particularly wretched situation. Even though they had fought fiercely for their country during the war, upon their return to the Soviet Union many were imprisoned or killed. In the eyes of Stalin, "any Soviet citizen—soldier or civilian—who had caught even a glimpse of life outside Russia without the guidance of political [representatives] was no longer trustworthy."[47] Stalin feared that his citizens would not be obedient to the communist way of life once they had been exposed to other lifestyles.

Refugees whom author Douglas Botting calls the "hard-core DPs" numbered nearly two million. These were the people who had no home to which they could (or would) go. They began gathering in central Europe soon after the war, "a horde of gaunt, ragged people . . . men, women, children and gigantic bundles."[48] To accommodate these displaced people, the Allies set up DP camps, where inmates were assigned by nationality. These were supposed to be temporary refuges, but for some "temporary" turned into years.

The camps were run by the UNRRA— the United Nations Relief and Rehabilitation Agency. This agency had been organized in

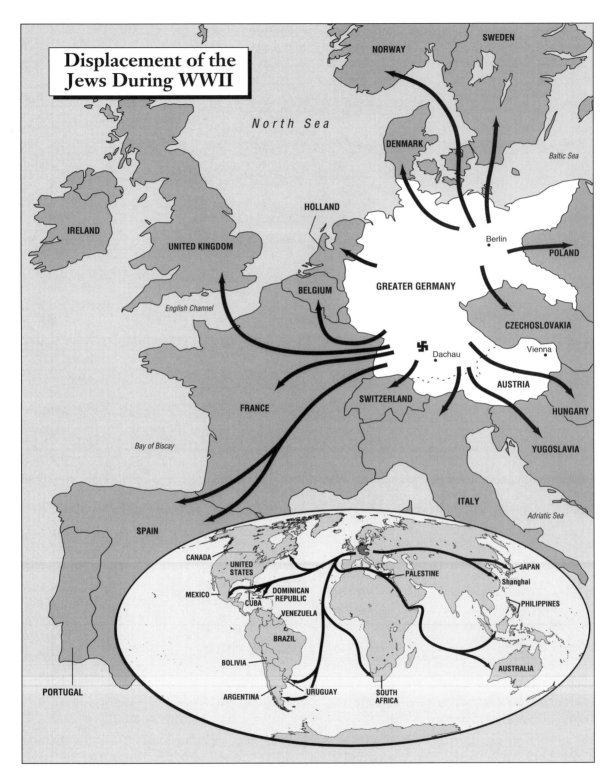

Displacement of the Jews During WWII

North Sea

SWEDEN

NORWAY

DENMARK

Baltic Sea

IRELAND

UNITED KINGDOM

HOLLAND

Berlin

POLAND

BELGIUM

GREATER GERMANY

English Channel

CZECHOSLOVAKIA

Vienna

Dachau

FRANCE

SWITZERLAND

AUSTRIA

HUNGARY

Bay of Biscay

YUGOSLAVIA

ITALY

Adriatic Sea

SPAIN

CANADA

UNITED STATES

PALESTINE

JAPAN

MEXICO

DOMINICAN REPUBLIC

Shanghai

CUBA

VENEZUELA

PHILIPPINES

BRAZIL

BOLIVIA

AUSTRALIA

PORTUGAL

ARGENTINA

URUGUAY

SOUTH AFRICA

1943 to deal with what the Allies knew would be a tremendous refugee problem. It was funded by forty-four nations who were fighting against Germany. UNRRA worker Kathryn Hulme lived with the DPs and worked at a camp called Wildflecken. It was her job not only to settle people into the camp, but also to see that fifteen hundred DPs per week were repatriated—reestablished as citizens in their home countries. Despite the conditions at home, recalls Hulme, most of the DPs in her camp were anxious to return, "even when the stay-behinds goaded them about Russians wait-ing to receive them into boxcars labeled for Siberia. For better or worse, their peaceful faces said, we are going home where we belong."[49]

Life in a DP Camp

Managing the camps was an overwhelming job. There were too many displaced persons, and their problems were enormous. Many were mentally unstable, had recurring nightmares, depression, and distrusted authority—even the military personnel trying to help them. Others suffered from physical illnesses caused by malnutrition

A group of Jewish children march in a displaced persons camp in suburban Berlin, Germany. The overcrowded conditions in these camps led to chronic food shortages and sanitation problems.

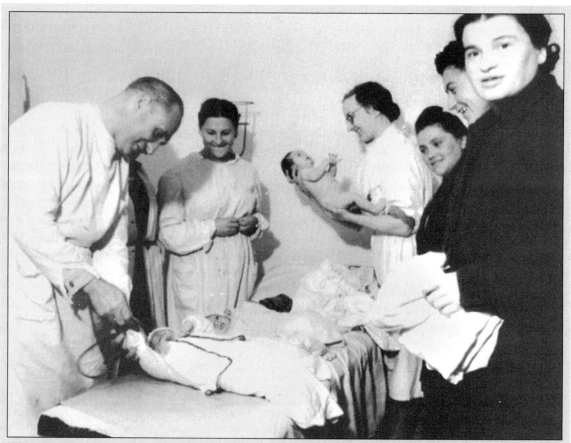

The baby clinic in the DP camp in Zeilsheim, Germany. Many survivors regarded it as a duty to have children to replace the millions who died at the hands of the Nazis.

and rampant disease during the war. Food shortages were acute, making hunger a constant fact of life.

In the first weeks that the DP camps were open, most residents were too weak, ill, and exhausted to complain about the conditions. They ignored the barbed wire surrounding the camps and the armed guards who kept residents from leaving without specific destinations and proper papers. Major Irving Heymont, director of the Landsberg DP camp in Germany, wrote in despair to his wife about conditions there: "The camp is filthy beyond description.

Sanitation is virtually unknown. . . . With few exceptions the people . . . appear demoralized beyond hope of rehabilitation. They appear to be beaten both spiritually and physically."[50]

Allied armies and international relief agencies were not prepared to deal with the vast numbers of homeless, ill, depressed, and starving people. Repatriating them created a quagmire of paperwork that prevented many from returning home even though they were ready. For them, the wait seemed endless; life in the camps was dull and depressing. Their situation seemed little better than it had in prisoner-of-war or concentration camps.

The longer term refugees tried hard to make the camps like homes and communities. Women partitioned rooms in the bunkhouses with sheets, allowing some privacy for friends or family groups. Men organized clothing and supply warehouses to look like department stores. Tradesmen and professionals such as lawyers, tailors, or barbers offered their services. Camp newspapers and political groups were established. Still, it was far from home.

One positive moment for Jewish DPs came in October 1945 when David Ben-Gurion, one of the leaders trying to build a Jewish homeland in Palestine, visited the camps. "Nothing that had yet happened had given the displaced persons such a boost to their morale, such a conviction that now it was only a question of waiting a little while longer"[51] for release from the camps, wrote Rabbi Judah Nadich. Ben-Gurion spoke at a DP camp in Landsberg, Germany, near the prison where Adolf Hitler had written *Mein Kampf*, his autobiography and blueprint for the Holocaust. The speech was a message of hope to survivors:

> I come to you with empty pockets. I have no certificates for you. I can only tell you that you are not abandoned. You are not alone. You will not live endlessly in camps like this. All of you who want to come to Palestine will be brought there as soon as it is humanly possible. I bring you no certificates—only hope.[52]

The Scathing Report of the Harrison Commission

In the United States, President Harry S. Truman had received reports of such horrid conditions in the DP camps that he thought they must be exaggerated. To find out the truth, he asked his longtime associate Earl Harrison, dean of the University of Pennsylvania Law School, to visit the camps and give him an honest appraisal. The report Truman received in August 1945 shocked him, and his concern was reported throughout the world. In his conclusion, Harrison said: "We [the U.S. government] appear to be treating the Jews as the Nazis treated them, except that we do not exterminate them. . . . One is led to wonder whether the German people seeing this are not supposing that we are following or at least condoning Nazi policy."[53]

Truman immediately sent a cable to General Dwight Eisenhower, commander of American forces in Europe. He told the general to give priority to helping those people who had suffered most find homes and get reestablished. DPs remaining in the camps should be treated with dignity and care. "We must make clear to the German people that we thoroughly abhor Nazi policies of hatred and persecution,"[54] Truman stressed.

Eisenhower was at first resentful of the report. To him, the Jewish DPs seemed unappreciative of the food and housing the Allies were providing. Having concentrated on military strategy and battle campaigns during the war, the general had little understanding of what the Jews had endured in the Holocaust. Even years later, after he became president of the United States, when a group of survivors presented him with a plaque showing their gratitude to the "Liberator of Auschwitz," Eisenhower asked in all innocence, "By the way, where *is* Auschwitz?"[55]

To confirm the Harrison Report, Eisenhower made a personal inspection of certain camps, something he had not had time to do in the chaos of postwar Europe. What he

General Patton's Anti-Semitism

One of the greatest generals in American history was also a virulent anti-Semite. General George Smith Patton, a 1909 graduate of West Point Military Academy, became famous in World War II for his daring raids with tanks.

"Old Blood and Guts," as he was known, fought in three major battle areas during the war. Patton commanded the U.S. Fifth Army during the invasion of North Africa, the U.S. Seventh Army at the attack on the island of Sicily, and the U.S. Third Army during the capture of Germany, which ended World War II in Europe. After the war, he served with the U.S. Army of Occupation in Europe, helping to organize the DP camps and to rebuild Germany from the rubble of war.

Patton's anti-Semitism was born during his youth in southern California. But it was while he was serving with the occupation forces that his hatred of Jews came to the surface. On August 31, 1945, in a letter to his wife, Patton wrote, "Actually the Germans are the only decent people left in Europe." In a later reference, he called the wife of an important official in the American government, "a very Jewy Jewess."

Patton's own diary entry contains some of his most blatant remarks. Infuriated by the Harrison Report, which described the deplorable conditions in the DP camps, Patton grudgingly accompanied General Eisenhower on his inspection tour of the Feldafing camp in August 1945. Patton was prepared to prove Harrison wrong. In his diary he wrote:

Harrison is ignorant of the fact that if [the DPs] were not kept under guard they would not stay in the camps, would spread over the country like locusts, and would eventually have to be rounded up after quite a few of them had been shot and quite a few Germans murdered and pillaged.

Patton vented his irritation with Harrison and others who, he said, "believe that the Displaced Person is a human being, which he is not, and this applies particularly to the Jews, who are lower than animals." He was also known to have called Jewish DPs "a sub-human species without any of the cultural or social refinements of our time." No ordinary people, he said, "could have sunk to the level of degradation these have reached in the short space of four years."

Old Blood and Guts was spared from having to deal with the DPs much longer after his camp inspection. He died in December 1945 of injuries suffered in an automobile accident in Germany. He is buried in a U.S. Army cemetery in Hamm, Luxembourg.

General George S. Patton.

Generals Eisenhower and Patton (behind Eisenhower) tour the displaced persons camps at Feldafing, Germany. The two had very different reactions to conditions at the DP camps. Eisenhower was appalled and demanded immediate reforms. Viciously anti-Semitic, Patton had little sympathy, calling Jews "a subhuman species."

saw convinced him that Harrison's observations were correct. Most upsetting to him was the fact that within a few yards of these miserable camps, German civilians—the perpetrators and bystanders during the Holocaust—were living in relative comfort, much as they had before the war.

Immediately Eisenhower ordered reforms within the camps. Barbed wire was taken down. Military armed guards were replaced by unarmed Jewish patrols. Food rations were increased. These orders met with resistance from some members of the general's lower staff, who considered the Jews to be demanding, uncooperative "wheeler-dealers," but eventually changes were made. Wrote Eisenhower in a concluding report, "I do not know when the stateless Jews will

be given a permanent home. It is my aim, until that time, to make it possible for them to lead a normal and useful life."[56]

Pressure now began to mount from worldwide Jewish and humanitarian agencies to step up the dreadfully slow rate at which DPs were being released from the camps. Palestine's doors remained closed, the United States and other countries had strict immigrant quotas, and thousands of survivors dared not go back to their homelands. But neither could they remain in DP camps indefinitely. President Truman felt the pressure intensely and responded with sympathy for Jews seeking a national homeland. His report recommended "the immediate admission of 100,000 Jews into Palestine," and added, "The transference of

But Where Were All the Jews?

When Helen Waterford was liberated from the work camp at Kratzau, Czechoslovakia, on May 9, 1945, she weighed seventy pounds and was covered with lice. Nevertheless, she set out on foot for Holland, where she had left her daughter, Doris, in hiding more than two years earlier. In her autobiography, *Commitment to the Dead*, written forty years after the war, she writes: "I still was not aware that all of central Europe had been involved in the fighting, that the cities and towns were mostly rubble, that there was no train travel, no electricity, and that all bridges had been destroyed. . . . All those people were on the road just as we were, trying to get home."

By May 20 Helen had gotten to Pilsen, on the German border, where the Americans were establishing the first DP camp:

> We [Helen and a fellow Kratzau inmate] made our way to this camp where about 400 people already were occupying the gymnasium. There were no beds, but clean blankets were distributed. . . . The people who shared this hall with us were primarily former slave workers, not too well nourished either, but not as emaciated as we were. . . . We were the only Jews in this group, and we could not believe it. Where were all the others?

It would be some time before Helen understood why there were so few Jews: because six million had been killed in the Holocaust. To her sorrow, she also began to realize that the lessons of the Holocaust had not been learned: "The fact that we were given larger amounts of food nearly caused a revolution, and anti-Semitic remarks abounded. . . . We had just escaped death, and others had been saved from slavery, yet here we were starting all over."

On June 1, Helen joined a truck convoy, the only means of transportation west. After two days, the convoy stopped at another DP camp at Leipzig, in East Germany. Here the refugees were sprayed with DDT, a toxic chemical that killed lice. Observed Helen: "This camp consisted of hundreds of tents and many large brick buildings, said to house 2,500 or more displaced persons. But—and this fact became more and more upsetting—there were not more than 30 Jews."

---

these unfortunate people should now be accomplished with the greatest dispatch."[57]

Desperately Seeking a Life

Despite the president's statement and the pressure from humanitarian groups, conditions in the camps remained bleak. One of the ugliest aspects was the recurrence of anti-Semitism. For a time after Eisenhower's investigation, DPs were allowed to live outside the camps in surrounding communities. But soon they were threatened and stones were being thrown at their homes, so they returned to the camps, where they felt safer. By 1947, even though thousands had left, one million displaced persons still remained in the camps.

For many, the promise of finding work abroad was their only hope. Having a job, no matter how menial, was a ticket out of the DP camp. But with millions of soldiers returning home to flood the job market, work was scarce. Most employers did not need foreign laborers, and so the DP camps were the last places they looked. Writes Kathryn Hulme, "The more highly educated the DP, the more absolute was his hopelessness. One Ukrainian doctor wept like a child when he was rejected from a scheme calling for hard-rock miners for Canada."[58]

The same fear that kept countries from admitting Jews during the Holocaust now kept them from admitting displaced persons from the camps. None of the countries that were in a position to take DPs, such as Australia, Canada, Great Britain, or the United States, seemed especially anxious to accept the war-ravaged refugees. "The last chapter in the Nazi persecution of the Jews," notes observer Robert Ross, "was written in the DP camps and in the emigration of survivors during the years after the war in Europe."[59]

President Truman was one of the best friends the DPs had in high places.

4 Heading to America

Of the 300,000 Jews who survived Hitler's concentration camps, approximately two-thirds fled to Palestine after the war, even though Jewish immigration there was at first illegal. The second largest number, nearly 72,000 survivors, headed for the United States. Another 16,000 went to Canada, 1,000 to Great Britain, and the remainder stayed in Europe. Nowhere were they welcomed with enthusiasm.

"The determined refusal of every Allied government to open the doors of its lands for more than token quotas of Jews was a traumatic shock for those who remained alive after the war ended,"[60] writes historian Abram Sachar. What had kept many victims alive in the death camps, adds survivor Elie Wiesel, was the dream of living in peace upon their release. Now the dream seemed only that. Foreign governments seemed deaf to the immigration pleas of survivors.

"None is too many,"[61] responded a Canadian official, when asked how many Jewish refugees his country could take. Labor unions, patriot groups, and other American organizations cried loudly that they did not want their country flooded with cheap labor. Even those who favored immigration cautioned that it must proceed slowly and carefully. An official of the American Friends Service Committee, an immigration group, said:

Now that immigration to this country is not a matter of actual rescue from persecution or danger, we feel that plans for immigration should be given careful consideration and weighed against all possible alternatives of return to the native country, remaining in the country of current residence, or possible migration to other countries.[62]

"The Buck Stops Here"

"The buck stops here," read the sign on President Truman's desk. It was one of the mottos by which he lived. No matter how thorny a problem, Truman was not afraid to take a stand, to take action. The refugee issue was no exception. In fact, the president was one of the best friends the DPs had in high places. He was sympathetic to survivors and had little patience with his own cabinet, whom he called "the striped pants boys." "They [don't] care enough," he complained to the president of the American Jewish Congress, "about what happen[s] to the thousands of displaced persons."[63]

Several times after he became president, Truman had taken bold steps to help survivors. When anti-Semitism and communism caused many returning survivors to flee Eastern Europe, Truman stepped in. He ordered the borders of the American zones of occupation in Germany and Austria opened to Jews who were trapped in Eastern Europe and the Balkan countries. He kept a constant watch on the DP camps after the Harrison Report, to be certain they were run like shelters rather than Nazi strongholds. He put pressure on the British government to allow greater immigration into Palestine. His order of December 22, 1945, granted special treatment to DPs who wanted to enter the United States, and some 22,950 displaced persons arrived—15,478 of them Jews.

Truman's Tower of Strength

Helping to form Truman's ideas of how the Jewish immigrant problem should be handled was his administrative assistant, David K. Niles. Niles had previously served President Franklin D. Roosevelt and had established a reputation for himself in dealing with the Jewish refugee problem. A Russian Jewish immigrant, Niles was a very quiet man who wanted no part of the public spotlight. Yet he wielded tremendous power over congressmen and politicians in Washington.

Niles had recommended that Truman appoint Earl Harrison to study the situation in the DP camps. When people criticized Truman for moving too slowly to help Jewish refugees, it was Niles who calmed them down. When American Jewish leaders complained that Truman was playing into the hands of "Arab dictators in the desert" with regard to Jewish settlement in Palestine, Niles convinced them to trust the president. "Niles was the eyes, ears, and

even, to some extent, whipping boy for the President,"[64] writes Abram Sachar.

The Immigration Law of 1948

One of the hottest issues facing President Truman was whether to increase the quota or number of immigrants who could enter the United States. American Protestant and Catholic organizations wanted to admit 400,000 DPs over a four-year period. More conservative politicians wanted stiff restrictions on who might enter. They said 40 percent of the visas should go to people like the Poles, whose home country had been taken over by a foreign power. Another 30 percent would be issued to farmers. Last on the list were people who had relatives in the United

David K. Niles was assigned to implement Truman's plans to allow 22,950 displaced persons to enter the United States. Niles continued to petition Congress to pass a bill allowing more Jews to immigrate.

States who would sponsor them—guarantee to take care of them until they could become established. Jews were not a priority.

Those weren't the only restrictions proposed by Congress. Eastern Europeans applying for visas had to prove that they had entered Western Europe after September 1, 1939, the day World War II began, and thus had truly been displaced by the war. Anyone entering before that date did not qualify. In the face of such overwhelming regulations, many DPs sought citizenship in other countries, where the requirements were not so strict.

Hoping to pass a law that would increase the immigration quota, Truman asked Niles to put pressure on members of Congress. A bitter struggle followed. One reason lawmakers were reluctant to pass the bill was the fear of communism that prevailed in the United States in the late 1940s and early 1950s. Anyone suspected of communist leanings was the object of severe harassment or even imprisonment. Only a small number of Jewish DPs were communists, but their presence did much to slow passage of the bill and to restrict the number of Jews who were allowed to enter.

At last, on June 25, 1948, the law passed, but not in the form Truman wanted. It allowed 200,000 immigrants to enter the

Displaced persons depart Germany for the United States under President Truman's 1945 directive that expedited immigration of displaced persons into the United States.

Communism and the Cold War

At the end of World War II, Allied leaders divided Germany into four sectors, or "occupation zones." Great Britain, France, the United States, and the Soviet Union each occupied one of the zones. By occupying Germany, the Allies hoped to stabilize Germany, help establish a new government, and assist the people in rebuilding their country.

In the Soviet zone of occupation, a communist government was set up. Soviet dictator Joseph Stalin at first agreed to hold free elections in East Germany, but he later broke this promise, as well as several others he had made with the other Allies. This was the beginning of the Cold War, a war of words between the free-world Allies and the communist countries that lasted more than three decades.

The German capital of Berlin lay in the East German zone of occupation, where the communists had control. Like the rest of Germany, Berlin was divided into four sectors. The three that were under the control of the free-world countries were like an island in a communist sea.

At first, American troops and their Allies had no trouble passing through East Germany to get to their sectors of Berlin. But by 1948 relations had become so tense that the Soviets blocked all road, rail, and water routes into the western part of the city. West Berlin was blockaded—cut off from food, fuel, and supplies. On July 26, Allied pilots began the largest airlift in world history, dropping supplies to the stranded citizens.

Finally in 1949 the Soviets agreed to lift the Berlin blockade, but with it came the lowering of the "Iron Curtain." This imaginary curtain of iron separated the communist countries of Central and Eastern Europe—among them East Germany, Poland, Hungary, and Czechoslovakia—from the democratic or free countries of Western Europe.

As the Cold War grew colder, so did living conditions in the communist countries. Poverty, pollution, and despair gripped the people throughout the 1960s and 1970s. Not until the late 1980s did communism begin to crumble in Eastern Europe. After more than forty years of division, East and West Germany were united again in 1990. The Cold War was over.

country over the next two years, but the stiff restrictions against who could enter remained. The president called the law "flagrantly discriminatory against Jews."[65] A similar statement came from William Haber, Jewish Adviser to the U.S. Army in Europe. He said the act was "the most anti-Semitic bill in U.S. history."[66]

Nevertheless, America's doors opened a little wider. In the four years that followed, 365,223 displaced persons entered the United States. Only 16 percent of them were Jews, however. Half were Roman Catholics, and many were admitted Nazi collaborators.

In 1949 the law was changed to make it less discriminatory against Jews. But by then, many survivors had made arrangements to go to other countries. In total, some 450,000 displaced persons found homes in the United States before the last

DP camp closed in 1952. Approximately 140,000 were Jewish Holocaust survivors. Still, in the end, the United States did more to help displaced persons than any other nation.

Assistance for New Immigrants

The problems the refugees faced when they arrived in America were enormous. Most had no money. They knew little or no English. Younger people, whose education had been interrupted or stopped by the war, had no training and few job skills. With the return of American servicemen, there was a housing shortage, and newcomers had a hard time finding places to live. In addition, Holocaust survivors were just beginning to recover mentally and physically. Those who had no nearby family in the United States had to turn elsewhere for support.

The Hebrew Sheltering and Immigrant Aid Society (HIAS) did most to help the Jewish DPs. This organization had been helping Jewish immigrants for decades before the Holocaust. To most new arrivals, they offered a small amount of money and assistance in finding work and housing. Often the housing was no more than a run-down boardinghouse or hotel, but it was the first time in years that many survivors had had a room of their own, and it seemed wonderful!

Ernest Michel, a German Jew, was sixteen years old when he was deported. He spent the next five years in various camps until he escaped in April 1945. Ernest was

An HIAS convoy leaves Paris for eventual arrival in the United States. The concentration camp survivors, eight men, seven women, and one child, are joining relatives in the United States.

one of the first DPs to enter the United States after the war, arriving in New York in 1946. Sensing right away that he didn't like New York, he contacted the National Refugee Service and asked for a transfer to Chicago, where he had a friend. They promised to pay his fare; the rest was up to him. Recalls Michel:

> I spoke very little English . . . and I felt that if I truly wanted to become an American I would have to get out of that [habit]. I went to Chicago because there was an army officer there who befriended me in Germany. . . . He invited me to come. He even offered to put me through school, but I didn't want him to do that."[67]

Settling into Life in America

Like many immigrants, Michel was proud, independent, and prepared to work extremely hard to better himself. A newspaperman in Chicago gave him a job at a paper in Port Huron, Michigan, despite his lack of English. Within a year, he was a regular columnist. Said Michel of his adjustment to the United States:

> It is possible that the fact that I had lost all my family but was still young and un-attached helped me, firstly to make the move to the USA at all, and secondly to adapt to life here. . . . It was a lot easier to [adapt] within a small, friendly community than it would have been in a big city. . . . In Port Huron, there were no other immigrants to speak of, and the population was pure American."[68]

David Bergman, who was deported to Auschwitz at age fourteen, immigrated to the United States in 1947. "I was looked at like I came from another world," he recalls.

"In their minds they had just seen the movies, the horrors." Age-wise, David was ready for high school, but he had missed the foundation of junior high while in the concentration camps. "So what do they do? They sent me to both. Talk about having a rough road, but I managed to keep up."[69]

This was the way of the immigrant survivors who came to America. They were determined. They were hardworking. They wanted passionately to rebuild their lives, to be successful, to create families who would become their legacy. One of these was Roman Ferber, who came to the United States when he was sixteen. Roman, a survivor of Auschwitz, was one of the youngest *Schindlerjuden*—Jews who were saved from death by Oskar Schindler, hero of the film *Schindler's List*. Said Roman many years later, "We tried to better ourselves. . . . Because we were in this tough time, I think it gave us an edge. You probably realize that many of [the survivors] did much better than the average person in the United States because we worked harder. We were accustomed to it."[70]

Most survivors adopted the United States with a fierce love, even though there were problems adjusting to the new land. Admits Auschwitz survivor Norbert Wollheim: "I have to say that, much as I love this country and grateful as I am to her, the Americans were very naive after the war. The excuse is that they were unprepared for the vast administrative burden the war would put on them, and the post-war period."[71]

Some survivors were unable to make the adjustment to a new culture, where few people understood what they had endured. Eighteen-year-old Madeline Deutsch was one of them. "Everybody was different," she later recalled. "They didn't go through what we went through. So I had nothing in common with any of the young people."[72]

Pursuing the American Dream

America was the land of freedom, where anyone who was willing to work hard could find success. But the shock of a totally new culture was frightening after everything the survivors had endured. One man admitted that he might have been more positive about emigrating if the United States had not been his only option. The fact that other countries would not admit him made him bitter about his new homeland from the outset.

German-born Auschwitz survivor Helen Waterford was among those who dreaded the move:

> The fact that I did not want to come at all gave me a hopeless feeling when I saw the Statue of Liberty for the first time. I cried because I wanted the ship to go home; I was frightened, deadly afraid of this country and its unknowns. I knew so little about America, other than its discovery by Columbus and something vague about the Indians. Most of my knowledge came from books by Karl May, who . . . admired the "American Spirit." That spirit made it possible for you to find work if you really wanted it, live in any city you pleased, and work without a permit. Most important—after five years I could apply for citizenship for Doris [her daughter] and me.[73]

Despite the quota and immigration problems, many Jews found the United States a much more welcome haven than

Members of two families reunited in Europe arrive in New York. For many survivors, reaching the United States was a long-held goal.

returning to their home countries in Europe. Even those who supported the establishment of a Jewish homeland in Palestine went themselves to the United States because they were tired of bloodshed, war, and persecution. Decades later, they are not sorry. "America gave us a home when we had none," writes David Chase, a survivor living in Connecticut. "America embraced us when we felt rejected. It gave us a feeling [of security] when we were stateless." Chase believes the letters *DP* should stand for "Delayed Pilgrim" rather than "Displaced Person." "We are proud to be Americans,"[74] he says.

To Palestine, the Promised Land

The First World War made the Zionist state possible. The Second World War made it essential. It persuaded the overwhelming majority of Jews that such a state had to be created and made secure whatever the cost, to themselves or to anyone else.[75]

T he anti-Semitism that had poisoned Europe over the centuries provided fertile ground for the seeds of the Zionist movement. Zionism began in Austria in the 1890s with Theodor Herzl, a Hungarian-born Jew. Herzl proposed a Jewish homeland in the region known as Zion—then called Palestine. The name came from a mountain near Jerusalem, in biblical times called Zion, which was a shrine of Judaism. Over the centuries, Zion became a symbol of the promised land for the Jews. Herzl's followers were called Zionists.

Since the end of World War I, Great Britain had controlled Palestine under the terms of the Balfour Declaration. That arrangement, drawn up in 1917 by British foreign secretary Arthur Balfour, would have a tremendous impact on future events in the Middle East. It read in part:

His Majesty's Government view with favor the establishment in Palestine of a

national home for the Jewish people, and will use their best [efforts to make it happen], it being clearly understood that nothing shall be done which may [harm] the rights of existing non-Jewish communities in Palestine.[76]

Zionist youth pose in front of an early version of the Israeli flag. Many survivors viewed the creation of a Jewish homeland in Palestine as the only guarantee against future persecution.

Strained Relations with the Arabs

The Balfour Declaration was a great boost to the Zionist movement. But it was also an impossible contradiction. Even before the ink had dried on the document, the British realized that it would be difficult—perhaps impossible—to create a Jewish homeland in Palestine without upsetting relations with the Arabs, who were a majority of the population. To complicate matters, with Hitler's rise to power in Europe, more and more Jews fled to Palestine. The Arabs objected loudly to Jewish settlement. And the British found themselves in an uncomfortable situation.

To try and stop the flow of immigration, the British government drew up the "White Paper" in 1939. This ruling limited to 1,500 the number of Jews who could immigrate to Palestine each month. But the White Paper backfired on the British. Fearing that if they waited, they might not be able to get into Palestine at all, European Jews now flocked to the promised land. Legal, as well as illegal, immigration soared.

The Arabs protested violently, while Britain walked a thin tightrope: trying to support the Balfour Declaration without arousing Arab ire. The British needed the

Illegal immigrants arrive at Haifa on the refugee ship Shivat Zion *on July 28, 1947. They are met by British soldiers who are under orders to keep them from disembarking.*

In Search of a Jewish Homeland

"If all the Jews wanted was a place where they could be safe," writes Paul Johnson in *A History of the Jews*, "it might be anywhere: Argentina, Uganda, Madagascar, for instance, were all proposed at one time or another. It was clear, however, that few Jews were interested in such schemes." What the Jews wanted was to return to the promised land, the land of Abraham, the father of the Hebrew nation. Genesis, the first book of the Bible, tells of God's promise to Abraham, whose name means "father of many nations": "The Lord made a covenant [promise] with Abram [Abraham] and said, 'To your descendants I give this land, from the river of Egypt to the great river, the Euphrates.'"

"This land" included what is today Israel, formerly Palestine. Beginning with Abraham's arrival, this was the land of the Hebrew people. For nearly a thousand years, Jews ruled the region. But by the mid–sixth century B.C., their power had begun to wane. From then until the birth of Jesus Christ, about the year 4 B.C., several groups controlled the area.

During the first century A.D., when Christ was alive, Romans controlled the country. Several times during this period, the Jews rebelled against Roman rule. In 70 A.D. the Romans crushed a Jewish uprising, conquered the holy city of Jerusalem, and destroyed the sacred Temple. Sixty-five years later, the Jews organized another revolt. This time they were driven from Jerusalem and warned never to return. Their land was taken over by the Arabs.

This was the beginning of the Diaspora, the scattering of the Jewish people. For nearly two thousand years they wandered the earth, rarely being accepted in countries where they tried to settle. Often they were treated very badly. During the fourteenth century, when the Black Plague claimed thousands of lives across Europe, Jews were blamed for poisoning the wells and causing the disease. During the fifteenth century Spanish Inquisition, when the Roman Catholic Church persecuted nonbelievers, Jews were among those who suffered the most. In 1492 they were expelled from Spain altogether.

Jews became the victims of prejudice again in sixteenth-century Germany during the Reformation, which resulted in the birth of the Protestant religion. Martin Luther, the outspoken founder of Protestantism, was a strong anti-Semite, and his influence in Germany was great. Jews began fleeing east, to Poland, where they formed the great Ashkenazi Jewish culture of Central and Eastern Europe. A new language was born among the Ashkenazim, a combination of the refugees' native German and the ancient Hebrew. Yiddish is still spoken today by many Jews worldwide.

Various waves of anti-Semitism continued to engulf Europe until, in the nineteenth and twentieth centuries, large numbers of Jews began immigrating to the United States. Those who remained behind became the victims of the Nazi Holocaust. It was the *She'erit Hapletah*, the "surviving remnant," who finally returned to the Jewish homeland in Palestine—the land that God had promised Abraham nearly four thousand years before—and helped to found what is today Israel.

Middle Eastern oil fields if they hoped to defeat Hitler's armies. To get that oil, they needed Arab support. In vain they tried to stop illegal Jewish entry into Palestine, but with each attempt, the situation worsened.

British Support for Zionism Weakens

A particularly unfortunate incident occurred on November 25, 1940, when 1,800 refugees arrived at the port of Haifa, in Palestine. The British imprisoned them on an old ship, the SS *Patria*, planning to deport them to an island in the Indian Ocean. But the Jews already in Palestine—the *Yishuv*—conceived a plan to aid the refugees. They would set fire to the ship, leaving the British no option but to let the refugees come ashore. Unfortunately, the explosive they used was too powerful. It destroyed the *Patria*, killing 240 passengers and 50 crew members. The British imprisoned those who survived.

Throughout the war, Jews continued their attempts to reach Palestine. And Britain continued to walk the tightrope. In 1944 tensions reached the explosive point between the British and the *Yishuv*. Members of a Jewish extremist group, the Lehi, assassinated Lord Moyne, a minister in the British government who was a close friend of Prime Minister Winston Churchill. An outraged Churchill warned the Jews:

> If our dreams for Zionism should be dissolved in the smoke of the revolvers of assassins and if our efforts for its future should provoke a new wave of banditry worthy of the Nazi Germans, many persons like myself will have to reconsider the position that we have maintained so firmly for such a long time.[77]

After the Lord Moyne incident, Churchill never recovered his zeal for Zionism. With

After the assassination of Lord Moyne by the Jewish extremist group Lehi, British prime minister Winston Churchill distanced himself and the British government from the Zionists.

the end of the war in 1945, the *Yishuv* pressured the British to end the White Paper quota. Churchill put them off, implying that he had other business of greater importance. It was clear that the British were tired of wrestling with the Palestinian problem. In a July memo concerning the creation of a Jewish state, Churchill wrote, "I am not aware of the slightest advantage that has ever accrued to Great Britain from this painful and thankless task."[78]

With Churchill's defeat in the July elections, a new government came to power in Great Britain. Ernest Bevin, the foreign secretary, opposed further Jewish settlement in Palestine. He promised to resist any actions on the part of the Jews "to ride roughshod over Arab and Moslem rights." At one point, Bevin pretended to be concerned that so many Jews were leaving Europe and their "ancestral lands where they had lived for centuries."[79] In truth, Bevin was not upset to see the Jews go, only to see them go to Palestine. His anti-Semitic attitude made the delicate situation in the promised land even harder to handle.

The Desperation of the Displaced People

In the summer of 1945, about fifty thousand Jews lived in Germany and Austria. Over the next eighteen months, anti-Semitic terror in Eastern Europe forced thousands more to flee there. As a result, the number of Jews in the DP camps quadrupled. American occupation zones were flooded with refugees hoping to find a safe haven. Vienna, Austria, became the checkpoint for eastern Jews trying to get to Palestine. There they could get the necessary papers for travel and make their way to Mediterranean ports, to begin the desperate voyage.

The Harrison Report on the DP camps had a big impact on illegal immigration. It drew attention to the horrid conditions in the camps and recommended that a hundred thousand Jews be admitted to Palestine at once. Britain promptly rejected the proposal. Foreign Minister Bevin made it clear that any solution "had to start with the premise that most of the Jews would remain in Europe, and that Palestine was not to be considered as a possible Jewish homeland."[80]

Nevertheless, most DPs were "filled with one longing—to go home."[81] Out of 22,000 questioned in the camps, 21,388 said they wanted to go to Palestine. "The overwhelming lesson the Jews had learned from the Holocaust," writes historian Paul Johnson, "was the imperative need to secure for themselves a permanent, self-contained and above all sovereign refuge where if necessary the whole of world Jewry could find safety from its enemies."[82]

The "Going Up"

Illegal immigration into Palestine never would have worked without the determination of the *Yishuv* to keep the doors open, despite White Paper restrictions. As far back as the 1920s, the *Yishuv* formed the *Haganah*, the Jewish national defense organization, to protect themselves from Arab attack. During and after the war, *Haganah* helped European Jews wishing to go to Palestine, to acquire money, food, clothing, and the necessary papers. They also plotted the most secret routes from Eastern and Central Europe, arranged truck and train transportation, and located ships that would carry the refugees across the Mediterranean Sea.

They were assisted in their planning by a group called *Bricha*, the Hebrew word for "escape." *Bricha* helped the refugees at border crossings, once *Haganah* had gotten the escape under way. The Poles benefited most from *Bricha*. With anti-Semitism facing them upon their return home, thousands of survivors simply turned around and fled back across the border to Central Europe. Some headed to the American Zone of Occupation; others to groups like *Haganah* that could help them get to Palestine. The Polish government, aware that many of these Jews might be assets to the country, tried to keep them from leaving, but with *Bricha*'s help, they escaped.

It wasn't easy. Ephraim Dekel, director of *Bricha*, describes the hazards of a border crossing through the Alps:

> We . . . had to start traveling over remote Alpine passes where we would not be likely to be found out. . . . During most of the

year the mountain trails were blocked by heavy snow. The few passes which we found were criss-crossed by mountain streams so that we had to set up temporary "bridges."

We did not know whether we were justified in exposing old people, or women and children, to the hazards of crossing the snow-bound Alps, especially since each trip had to be made after dark. We therefore planned to use these trails only for moving young people and other individuals who were physically fit for the rigors of clandestine border crossings and for the "illegal" journey by boat to Palestine.[83]

Beginning in 1937, the *Yishuv* had organized the *Mossad Aliyah Bet*, the "Illegal Immigration Organization." *Mossad*, another arm of *Haganah*, was responsible for the sea portion of the refugees' journeys. This was particularly dangerous work, for the British Royal Navy did everything in its power to keep the Jews from landing in Palestine. Sometimes the navy would stop refugee ships and demand that they turn back. Other times there would be open fighting between *Mossad* and the British navy.

Illegal immigrants stare out from the windows of their damaged vessel after their arrival in Israel. The mesh screen they are erecting is meant to deter the British from boarding their vessel.

The illegal immigration movement was called the *Aliyah Bet*. In Hebrew, *aliyah* means "going up to the land" (in this case Palestine) and *bet* is the second letter of the alphabet—implying a second or alternate (illegal) way of "going up to the land." From the time the war ended until the state of Israel was created in 1948, more than 70,000 Jews attempted the *aliyah*. All together, from 1944 to 1948, 200,000 Jews made the journey—legal or illegal—from Eastern and Central Europe to Palestine.

Spring 1946: The Flood of Refugees Builds

It wasn't just the anti-Semitism of the Polish people that made Jews flee to the promised land. It was also the situation in the DP camps. Not only did refugees suffer from lack of food and decent living conditions, they soon became very frustrated with the snail's pace at which the politicians were moving to help them. They were tired of waiting with no hope in sight.

In May 1946, as the *aliyah* increased in numbers, American journalist I. F. Stone decided to join a group of emigrants to see what the trip would be like. To protect the routes and actions of *Haganah*, Stone promised not to use names or locations that would give away secret information to the British. The veteran journalist was "aware of the trials which lay ahead," he says. "I had heard of the dangers and delays which beset the underground route to Palestine, but there was no apprehension among my fellow voyagers. . . . Ahead somewhere were security, freedom and a new home."[84]

At last, after weeks of harrowing travel, Stone's ship neared the port of Haifa. Immediately, "the refugees cheered and began to sing *Hatikvah*, the Jewish national anthem. . . . People jumped for joy, kissed and hugged each other on the deck. So singing, we moved into the arms of the waiting British."[85] Fortunately for Stone and his fellow travelers, the British allowed them to stay in Palestine. But from that time on, Britain warned that all "illegals" caught by the Royal Navy would be sent to Cyprus, an island in the Mediterranean Sea, just north of Palestine.

Stone's group was lucky. A refugee named Shmuelik, who was aboard another boat, was among the unfortunates who were refused entry. The group arrived exhausted, Shmuelik said, from a storm that had made them all seasick. In Haifa, they were put onto trucks and told that soon they would be taken to Cyprus. But when the time came to board the boat, the Jews refused to get out of the trucks.

> They [the British] tried to get us out by force—and it was no easy task for them. We were empty-handed, but we held on to one another and attached ourselves to the sides of the truck. The English tried to separate some of the girls by pulling their hair, but clenched fists sprang out of our mass of people and flew like bullets. . . . By the force of blows of rifle-butts and sticks, the British tore off body by body from the solid mass. Four soldiers were needed to drag each of us to the boat.[86]

The scene was similar when the ship finally reached Cyprus. But in the long run, such British actions did little more than delay *aliyah*. During the next two years, fifty-six more shiploads of refugees tried to immigrate illegally.

The Plight of the *Exodus*

The most famous voyage of the *aliyah* began in Sète, a port near Marseilles in southern France, in the summer of 1947, aboard an old Chesapeake Bay cruise ship renamed *Exodus 1947*. The passengers were 4,554 men, women, and child survivors of the Holocaust, who were heading doggedly for the Jewish homeland.

This time the British did not wait for the boat to dock before they turned it away. As the ship neared Palestine, two British navy vessels rammed the side of the *Exodus*, causing severe damage. Members of the British crew boarded the boat and a battle began. Three hours later, with two refugees and an *Exodus* crewman dead, the Jews surrendered.

But the fight had only begun. What the refugees expected was to be taken to Cyprus. What they got was the news that they were being shipped back to France. Like cattle, the British herded them into cages on three boats—one witness called them "floating prisons"—and returned them to Sète. Upon arrival, only 130 refugees disembarked. The French, not wishing to get involved in this thorny problem, refused to admit anyone into the country who did not get off voluntarily.

The British now faced an embarrassing showdown. If they relented and allowed the Jews to go back to Palestine, they risked the wrath of the Arabs. They also risked losing control of the immigration situation. British foreign secretary Ernest Bevin decided to take a hard stand. He and other cabinet members ordered the Jews returned—to Germany.

The outside world and survivors alike were shocked and enraged. Even Winston Churchill condemned Bevin and the cabinet for what he called "callous hostility."[87] Nevertheless, on September 8, 1947, the homeless Jews arrived in Hamburg. The first two ships landed peacefully, and passengers disembarked. But those on the third ship refused to move. They had to be teargassed and dragged, kicking and biting their guards, onto German soil.

Jewish immigrants leave the battle-damaged Exodus *after its seizure by the British navy. The British handling of this affair resulted in a public furor.*

Exodus: A Dream Twenty Centuries Old

The ship that left Sète, France, on the most famous voyage of the *aliyah* was not named by accident. The word *exodus* has a rich meaning in Jewish history. According to the Bible, Jacob—the grandson of Abraham, father of the Jewish people—had twelve sons. Each of these sons was the leader of a tribe of people, together known as the twelve tribes of Israel (for Jacob was also called Israel). These tribes were the beginning of the large Jewish nation.

So numerous did the people of Israel become that the king of Egypt feared they would overtake his land, so he made them his slaves. The Israelites suffered tremendously under the Egyptians and prayed to God for deliverance. The Bible says that God heard their prayers and answered by sending Moses to lead them out of Egypt. In Exodus, the second book of the Bible, God explained to Moses the promise that he made to Abraham and his descendants:

> I also established my covenant [promise] with them to give them the land of Canaan [Israel] where they lived as aliens. Moreover, I have heard the groaning of the Israelites, whom the Egyptians are enslaving, and I have remembered my covenant.

> . . . I am the Lord, and I will bring you out from under the yoke of the Egyptians. I will free you from being slaves to them, and I will redeem you with an outstretched arm. . . . And I will bring you to the land I swore with uplifted hand to give to Abraham, to Isaac and to Jacob. I will give it to you as a possession. I am the Lord.

Moses then led his people out of Egypt in the first exodus, or "mass departure," of Jews from a land that did not want them. Then, as in the 1947 exodus, they headed for the promised land of Canaan-Palestine-Israel. Moses and some of the Israelites never completed the long journey, just as many Holocaust survivors never completed the *aliyah*.

But their determination to settle the land that God promised to their ancestors is a moving story. So moving, in fact, that author Leon Uris used the 1947 exodus as the subject of his novel by that name, which later became a movie. In Uris's story, Karen, a teenage Holocaust survivor, is so inspired by the movement to settle Israel that she gives up the search for her missing parents in Europe to go on the *Exodus 1947* to Palestine. Karen becomes a symbol of the new land's spirit.

"We have no life in Europe or Germany," screamed one, "nowhere but Palestine."[88]

It was bad enough to return Holocaust survivors to Germany, the country of the perpetrators, but their housing was an outrage. One group was sent to a camp for liberated Allied prisoners of war. The other group was sent to Bergen-Belsen, the infamous Nazi concentration camp and typhus graveyard. Barbed wire and armed guards surrounded the camps. Most inmates refused to cooperate with their British captors. When asked for their names and nationalities, they cried only, "Palestine!"

Displaced persons in Bergen-Belsen, Germany, carry banners protesting the British decision to force the return of the Exodus *to Germany.*

As the months passed, the British guards became lax. Perhaps they were bored with their dismal tour of duty; or perhaps they felt guilty at the wrath the rest of the world was now heaping on the British. In any event, when the Jews began to leave the camps, no one stopped them. Within a year, the camps were empty of survivors, most of them headed toward Palestine to try again.

Establishing a Jewish State

People worldwide were now in sympathy with the plight of the Jewish DPs. Great Britain's reputation suffered greatly after the *Exodus* incident. The *aliyah* was making it difficult for the British to keep control of Palestine. Earlier in the year they had asked the newly formed United Nations to decide who should rule the country. UN representatives were present in Palestine when the *Exodus* passengers were put onto their floating prisons and returned to Europe. Wrote Abba Eban, later Israel's ambassador to the UN: "I could see that they [the UN representatives] were preoccupied with one point alone. If this were the only way that the British [rule] could continue, it would be better not to continue it at all."[89]

The United Nations realized that the only hope of settling the Palestinian problem would be a compromise. Each side was determined to win and was stopping at nothing to ensure a victory. Each side used political favors, trade-offs, business contributions, government loans, and personal connections. "The most unholy means were considered fair to settle the fate of the Holy Land," writes historian Abram Sachar acidly.[90]

At last, on November 29, 1947, the UN General Assembly adopted a resolution. It called for the partition of Palestine into an Arab state and a Jewish state. The holy city of Jerusalem would be an international zone, not controlled by either group. This resolution would become effective in May 1948, when the British control of Palestine was set to expire.

The UN proposal to partition Palestine pleased neither the British nor the Arabs. Britain's UN ambassador refused to vote on the matter. Representatives of several Arab nations walked out of the meeting. "The idea," writes Abba Eban, "was to settle Jews where Arabs were *not* in firm possession."[91] It was a decision that made sense on paper, but no sense in reality. Said Moshe Dayan, later Israeli minister of defense:

> We were happy that night, and we danced, and our hearts went out to every nation whose UN representative had voted in favor of the resolution. We had heard them utter the magic word "yes" as we followed their voices over the air-

waves from thousands of miles away. We danced—but we knew that ahead of us lay the battlefield.[92]

Living Out the UN Decision

President Harry Truman and a majority of Americans supported the partition. Great Britain and the Arab nations violently opposed it. In fact, in the months that followed, the British government refused to acknowledge or accept the partition at all. A certain segment of Americans also opposed it and worried about its impact on Arab relations. One influential oilman said that Truman's support for the decision had "extinguished the moral prestige of America" and had destroyed "Arab faith in her ideals."[93]

Survivors were ecstatic, but they did not intend to wait until the following May to resume emigration. They continued their dangerous mission despite the risks. Berl Levin, a teenage Holocaust survivor, arrived off the coast of Herzliyya in the dark of night. The warm reception he received made him joyous to be in Palestine. "We waited for the signal from the shore that it was safe to disembark," Levin recalls.

> I took to this country . . . like a duck to water. . . . We weren't surrounded by enemies any more—on the contrary, people here could not have been kinder to us. Everything was laid on for us, right down to toothpaste! We were treated like refugees from hell, and greeted like old friends—everybody wanted to hear our story.[94]

Journalist I. F. Stone reported that the refugees' desire to go to Palestine was simple and sincere. When he asked survivors what motivated them, one said, "I am a Jew. That's enough. We have wandered enough. We have worked and struggled too long on the lands of other peoples. We must build a land of our own."[95]

Not all survivors, however, were ecstatic about going to Palestine. They went because they saw no other option. Zdenka Novak was a Yugoslavian Jew who lost her husband, her sister, and her parents in the Holocaust. She survived as a partisan and remarried at war's end. The prospect of emigration "really was not at all an event of sheer enjoyment," she recalls, "although the mere thought of having got the chance to leave Tito's [the communist leader of Yugoslavia] realm was kind of comforting."

Three Jewish children are en route to Palestine after their liberation from the Buchenwald concentration camp.

In addition to personal concerns about emigrating, Zdenka says, "the pure and honest truth was that we both were not Zionists. It never occurred to me to think that a Jew must be a Zionist, one whose purpose in life is to go and live in Palestine."[96]

Still, the Holocaust and the settlement of Palestine were, as historian Paul Johnson puts it, "organically connected. The murder of six million Jews was a prime [cause] of the creation of the state of Israel." Ever since the Diaspora, Jews had been wandering, away from the hatred of their fellow human beings. Hitler's Final Solution, says Johnson, "was the last in the series of catastrophes which helped to make the Zionist state."[97]

The Birth of Israel

The United Nations' partition of November 30, 1947, sparked increasing waves of terrorism and violence throughout Palestine. In the month following the announcement of the partition, 489 people died, as fighting erupted between the Jews and the Arabs. "This Christmas week in the Holy Land," wrote an American journalist, "shepherds went armed, travelers to Bethlehem were shot at, and wise men stayed indoors."[98]

Tension in the country grew daily. Arabs, who outnumbered Jews two to one, "demanded to know why they should have to pay for Hitler's crimes."[99] Until the end of the war, the Jews had been peaceful in their settlement of Palestine. It was the Arabs who had defended their country with violence. But as time passed and the British failed to make good on their promise to establish a Jewish homeland, the Jews became more violent against the Arabs and the British as well.

Jewish Extremist Groups

At the center of the violence was *Haganah*, the organization that helped Jews escape from Europe. Not only did *Haganah* assist escapees, it was also the Jewish underground army in Palestine. Although the group carried on terrorist activities, members took care that their violence did not lead to deaths on either side. In addition to *Haganah*, two other Jewish extremist groups operated within the country. The two-thousand-member *Irgun* was headed by Holocaust survivor Menachem Begin, who later became prime minister of Israel. The Stern gang was smaller than *Irgun*, with about two hundred members. Although

Two members of Haganah *keep watch for Arab troop movements in Haifa after the formation of Israel.*

the three groups shared the same goals, there were many issues on which they did not agree; in fact, there was outright hatred among some members.

Begin and the *Irgun* were convinced that the British government would never remove White Paper restrictions on immigration to Palestine. They used this as a justification for attacking British agencies and units stationed in the Holy Land. "If we did not fight," Begin insisted, "we should be destroyed. To fight was the only way to salvation." [100]

The Stern gang was extremely violent, carrying on junglelike warfare within cities. "They tossed hand grenades into police stations, planted mines inside army posts, left bombs in train depots, tax offices and banks . . . machine-gunned policemen from rooftops and robbed banks and armored cars to finance their campaign of urban terror." [101] Often Stern and *Irgun* members disguised themselves in Arab garb or British military uniforms. These extremists gave little thought to who died in their attacks. Jews, Britons, and Arabs of all ages became their victims. During 1946 alone, 373 people died at their hands. Their purpose was to create continual havoc, until the British tired of dealing with the prickly Palestinian issue and abandoned the country.

Terrorism Becomes a Way of Life

Today, terrorist tactics are well-known. But in the late 1940s, they were new and brought considerable attention to the plight of the Jews. This "scientific use of ter-ror," writes historian Paul Johnson, "might be called a by-product of the Holocaust, for no lesser [event] could have driven even desperate Jews to use it." [102]

One of the worst attacks occurred on July 22, 1946, when *Irgunist* agents blew up the King David Hotel in the center of Jerusalem. The hotel was the headquarters for many top-ranking British officers. Later, *Irgunists* insisted that they had issued a thirty-minute warning, so people could leave the building safely. They claimed the warning was ignored or never given to people in the hotel. The result was that ninety-one Britons, Arabs, and Jews were killed in this

British soldiers search for bodies after the Irgunist *bombing of the King David Hotel in Jerusalem.* Irgunists *targeted the hotel because it was the headquarters for many British officers.*

action. Citizens and world leaders alike condemned the event, calling the action "criminal lunacy."[103]

British Reactions to Terrorism

The British, determined to control an increasingly chaotic situation, put curfews into effect and patrolled city streets with armored cars. Suspecting that the Jewish extremists were collecting guns and ammunition, they frequently made surprise raids and often uncovered substantial stashes of arms. After each terrorist act, the British brought in hundreds—sometimes thousands—of Jews for questioning.

When the British caught terrorists, their policy was to flog and hang them. *Irgun* adopted the same policy. After three *Irgun* members attacked a prison at Acre and freed 251 prisoners, both sides put the policy into practice. The *Irgun* members were captured, and Menachem Begin threatened to retaliate if they were killed. He got the opportunity. The *Irgunists* were hanged by the British on July 29, 1947. Within hours two British sergeants, Clifford Martin and Mervyn Paice, were hanged by *Irgun*.

This senseless act sickened the entire country, including the Jews, and caused the British to rethink their commitment to Palestine. It was time, they decided, to get out of the middle and let the Jews and the Arabs fight it out. When their Mandate—the agreement that originally gave them control of Palestine—expired in May 1948, they would not fight to keep control of the country.

The Violence Continues

On April 9, 1948, just a month before the Mandate expired, an incident occurred that finalized Britain's decision to get out of Palestine. It took place in the Arab quarrying town of Deir Yassin. This community of fewer than a thousand people had made an agreement not to fight with the Jews. But when two Jewish communities nearby were attacked by Arabs, the Stern gang retaliated. Their plan was to destroy Deir Yassin.

Irgun and *Haganah* joined Stern, on the agreement that the Arabs be given a chance to surrender before any fighting began. Instead, the Arabs decided to fight and were quite well prepared. At last, however, the Jews brought in a heavy machine gun and other arms against which the Arabs were helpless. A bloody massacre followed, in which approximately 250 Arabs died.

The world was outraged. British historian Arnold Toynbee was particularly outspoken, proclaiming the massacre a "typical act of Jewish ruthlessness." "The Jews were worse than the Nazis,"[104] he fumed. Over the next two months, large numbers of Arabs fled Palestine, for this and other reasons. The Arab population was reduced to 160,000 people, compared to the Jewish population of 600,000.

The British Leave Palestine

May 14, 1948, marked the end of British rule in Palestine and the birth of the Jewish State of Israel. Down went the British Union Jack; up went the white flag with the blue six-pointed Jewish star in the center. It was the first independent Jewish state in 1,878 years. A new term now emerged. No longer were the people *Yishuv*, or "Palestinian Jews." They were Israelis.

David Ben-Gurion, the nation's first prime minister, read the Scroll of Independence from the Tel Aviv Museum: "By virtue of our national and intrinsic [God-given] right, and on the strength of the resolution of the United Nations General Assembly, we hereby declare the establishment of a Jewish state in Palestine, which shall be known as the State of Israel."[105]

That night the fighting began. As the Palestinians had hoped, neighboring Arab countries now came to their aid. Egypt and Syria were the first to attack. Jordan, Lebanon, and Iraq soon joined the fight. Their intent, they said, was to "drive the Jews into the sea."[106] Most military experts predicted that they would.

Independence Brings War

The Arab countries that moved in to attack Israel when the British left now proclaimed a *jihad*—a holy war—against the Jews. The Arabs were united on one point: They did not want a Jewish state to be established in Palestine. But on nearly all other points they disagreed, often violently. This mistrust of each other, and the fact that each Arab country was secretly fighting to capture a piece of Palestine for itself, caused chaos and weakness among the troops. Rarely had Arabs helped other Arabs, and the likelihood of that happening in Palestine was slim.

Throughout history, Arabs had been conquerors, not negotiators. They did not operate by discussion or compromise. The division of Palestine was a perfect example—because it represented a type of compromise,

An Arab sniping post takes aim at a Jewish quarter in Jerusalem. Arabs and Jews continued fighting in spite of British attempts to secure a cease-fire.

(Left) Members of Haganah *defend their post in the Negev desert area of southern Palestine. (Above) Arab soldiers man a mobile gun, shelling Jewish positions.*

the Arabs refused to accept it. Jews, on the other hand, were negotiators. For two thousand years they had been the oppressed people and had gotten used to bargaining their way out of bad situations. No matter how unacceptable a compromise, they would take what they could get and plan to negotiate later for terms that were more acceptable.

Now, the tables were turning. Jews began fighting fiercely for their promised land. Arabs foresaw that they might have to

accept a hated compromise: the division of their country. Both sides began an intensive drive to sign up able-bodied young people to fight for their cause. *Haganah* provided the core of the new Israel Defense Forces (IDF). The Arabs sent many of their young people to neighboring Syria for a month, to train with the Syrian armed forces.

Under British control, the Arabs had not been allowed to maintain an army. This lack of training and preparedness put them at a great disadvantage against the Israelis, most of whom had been fighting for their lives during the Holocaust and were very determined survivors.

The Israelis had a definite psychological edge on the Arabs, a spirit they called *ain braira*, "no alternative." The Jews were fighting for the only chance they had to gain a homeland. If they lost, they were doomed to continue the Diaspora. "The Arabs," writes Abram Sachar, "never fully understood how powerful a weapon desperation could be."[107]

The Fight for the Major Cities

Even before the British left, fighting had raged in the Tel Aviv/Jaffa area. Jaffa had long been the largest city in Arab Palestine. In 1914 Jewish pioneers settled the sandy suburbs south of the city and soon this area—called Tel Aviv—was larger than Jaffa itself. According to the UN partition plan, the Arabs were to hold Jaffa, the Israelis Tel Aviv. But neither side was content with this arrangement. Whoever controlled Tel Aviv/Jaffa also controlled the roads north to the port of Haifa and south to the holy city of Jerusalem.

In the months leading up to independence, the Jews rained constant terror on Jaffa, and the Arabs did the same in Tel Aviv. The British, in their role as middlemen, shelled Jewish positions to stop the terrorist attacks. But the Jews got the upper hand, and ninety-six thousand Arabs fled the area in fear. By the time the British withdrew, only four-thousand Arabs were left in Jaffa. The Israelis had won the area.

Even though the UN resolution had said Jerusalem would be an "international city," both the Arabs and the Jews wanted control. As in Tel Aviv, the fight began even before the British pulled out of Palestine. The capital was not important militarily, but Jews and Arabs, as well as Christians, considered it the center of their religions—the holiest of cities. For that reason, both sides were prepared to fight to the death for control.

In the month following the end of the British rule, ten thousand shells exploded in Jerusalem's Old City. More than seventeen hundred soldiers and civilians died fighting for this holy shrine—children as well as adults. One nine-year-old boy who had been a messenger during the heaviest shelling of the city explained why he was not afraid. "I'm still four years away from Bar Mitzvah, and so small that as I crawl on my belly the big shells don't even see me."[108]

The Jews lost the battle for Jerusalem. On May 28, 1948, the Arabs took over the Old City, forcing the Jews into the newer section. Starvation became a serious problem, for supply routes up the hills into the Jewish section were controlled by the Arabs. But the Israelis held strong and vowed the defeat was temporary. They promised to recapture Old Jerusalem as soon as the rest of the country was secure.

War: A Series of Truces

The first round of Israel's War of Independence lasted less than a month. On June 11, a UN-supervised truce took effect. Count Folke Bernadotte, president of the Swedish Red Cross, was the mediator, whose job was to try to bring both sides together in peace.

The timing of the truce was perfect, for the Israelis were near the point of exhaustion. Their food supply was dangerously low, and they needed time to fortify themselves. During the truce, thousands of Jewish refugees streamed into the country, supplying much-needed manpower for the Israel Defense Forces.

The British continued to support the

Arabs, giving them arms and other supplies even after the Mandate expired. The Arabs and their British allies urged Bernadotte to revise the partition plan. They wanted him to take the southern portion of the Negev—a vast desert that the Israelis hoped to turn into farmland—away from the Jews and give it to the Egyptians. In exchange, the Jews would receive the western sections of Galilee—land they had already won during the fighting.

But the Jews did not intend to surrender the Negev without a fight, and so the already fragile truce was broken one month after it began. "When the fighting resumed on 9 July," writes historian Paul Johnson, "it quickly became apparent that the Israelis were in control."[109] Their goal was to eliminate Arab forces in the desert. They were also fighting for control of a major airport at Lydda, and for lands around Ramleh and Nazareth. Before they could accomplish their mission, another truce took effect, on July 18. This time the United Nations ordered, not asked, that the fighting stop.

During this truce, Count Bernadotte worked tirelessly with Arab and Jewish leaders to try to bring a permanent end to the fighting. But on September 17, it became clear just how far away from peace the two sides were, when Count Bernadotte and an assistant were assassinated by a Jewish terrorist group. The Israeli government was as shocked and outraged as the rest of the world.

Jewish firefighters hose down two buses set afire by Arab mortar shells in Jerusalem in 1948.

Jewish leaders now realized that they were going to lose the Negev unless they occupied it with force. On October 14, the third round of the war began, with Egyptians fighting Israelis in the Negev. Although other Arab countries talked about helping the Egyptians, leaders could not agree on an approach, and the Egyptians finally retreated.

By January 1949 the Israelis had captured an impressive amount of land and were clearly the victors in the War of Independence. On January 12, peace talks began and eventually armistices were signed, first with Egypt, then with Lebanon, Jordan, and Syria. Iraq was the only Arab country to hold out. The Arabs captured 14 areas that the partition originally had given to the Jews. The Israelis, on the other hand, conquered 112 villages that the partition had assigned to the Arabs. Fighting had ceased, but in reality, the Arab-Israeli conflict had only begun, and goes on to this day.

The Aftermath of War

"The war for independence and its successful outcome was to transform the historic image of the Jew,"[110] writes Abram Sachar. No longer would Jews be accused, as they had been in the Holocaust, of going passively like sheep to the slaughter. They had fought for and won a land of their own. No more were Jews the displaced people of the Diaspora; they were the people of Israel.

The end of the War of Independence brought a new flood of refugees to the infant nation. As soon as Chaim Weizmann took office as the new country's first president, the much-hated quota on immigration was

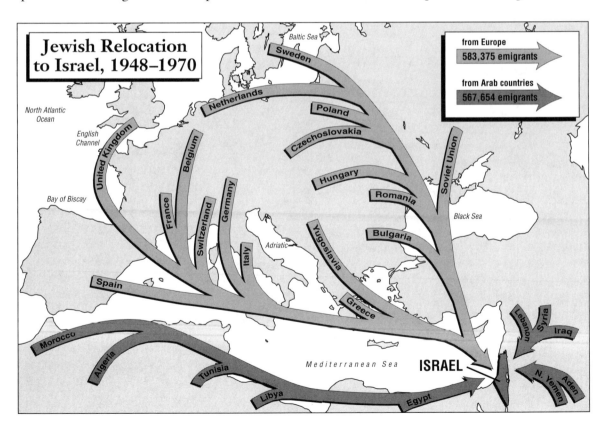

Jewish Relocation to Israel, 1948–1970

from Europe: 583,375 emigrants
from Arab countries: 567,654 emigrants

dropped completely. Jews were now free to emigrate from any country in the world to Israel. Soon the DP camps of Europe and the detention camps on Cyprus began emptying at a rapid rate. By the fall of 1949, ten thousand Jews a month were leaving for the promised land. The flood lasted through the end of 1950. On December 17, the Central Committee of Jewish Displaced Persons, which had helped refugees get to Israel, disbanded because it was no longer needed. Everyone had arrived who wanted to come.

That same year the Knesset, Israel's parliament, passed the 1950 Law of Return. This law gave every Jew the right to settle permanently in Israel. In 1954 another law was passed, granting citizenship to any Jewish immigrant. For many Holocaust survivors without a country, the chance to become a citizen with proper papers was a dream come true.

Strangers in Their Own Land

At war's end, the Jews living in Arab-held lands quickly fled to Israeli territory. But the Arabs remaining in Israeli-occupied lands became refugees in their own country. In most cases, there was not room for them in the remaining Arab-held sections of Israel. Because of long-standing friction and disagreement among Arabs of different nationalities, neighboring Arab countries also refused to take in the refugees. It would be too great an economic burden on their governments, leaders claimed. Major General Chaim Herzog, a veteran of the many Arab-Israeli conflicts, later made this observation: "It is sobering to reflect that just one day's Arab oil revenues, even in 1949, would have sufficed to solve the entire Arab refugee problem. But it was not to be." [111]

What *was* to be was a continuing series of skirmishes, some erupting into full-scale wars, between the Israelis and their displaced Arab

---

Chaim Weizmann and the New Israeli Government

Chaim Weizmann, a chemist who was born in what is now Belorussia, was the man chosen to become Israel's first president. From 1920 to 1931, Weizmann had served as president of the World Zionist Organization and participated in the discussions that led to the Balfour Declaration.

A longtime resident of England, he attended the historic conference in 1920 that awarded the Palestine Mandate to Great Britain. Again, from 1935 to 1946, Weizmann headed the World Zionist Organization and played a major role in helping Jewish refugees settle in Palestine. His influence as Israel's first president helped the tiny country get immediate recognition and financial aid from the United States.

The first meeting of the Knesset, the new Israeli parliament, was held in February 1949. Despite the ruling that Jerusalem was to be governed by an international group and that the Arabs already controlled the old section of the city, the Israelis proclaimed Jerusalem their capital. It was a defiant move, but no one disputed it.

---

neighbors. Today more than 17 percent of the population of Israel is not Jewish. Most of these people—some 750,000—are Arabs. Although peace negotiations looked promising in the mid-1990s, violence has since erupted many times.

In its Declaration of Independence, written in 1949, Israel promised to uphold "the full social and political equality of all its citizens without distinction of religion, race, or sex." It called upon "the Arab inhabitants of the State of Israel to preserve the ways of peace and play their part in the development of the State, on the basis of full and equal citizenship."[112]

Nearly fifty years later, preserving the peace still seems like an impossible dream. Israel was a nation conceived in violence, and that has remained its legacy. Over the years, some of the most violent activists have become national leaders or heroes. The two members of the Stern gang who murdered Lord Moyne in 1944 were praised as national heroes in 1975. Under military guard, their bodies were moved from obscure graves to graves of honor on Mount Israel. Another participant in the murder plot, Yitzhak Shamir, was chosen Speaker of the Knesset in 1977. Menachem Begin, one of the major leaders of *Irgun*, eventually became prime minister.

These Israelis were different types of Jews than the generations before them, who had relied on negotiation and compromise rather than fighting and violence. In the aftermath of the Holocaust, those Jews who survived were determined to take a stand against any further persecution of their people. They were prepared to fight to the death for their right to live in peace. The founding of Israel, writes historian Abram Sachar, "could not have been possible without the emergence of a new breed of men and women who had cast off the [meekness] of the Diaspora and whose combined talents for daring and tenacity matched the most [fearless] exploits of modern times."[113]

CHAPTER
7 Survivors Rebuild Their Lives

"Throughout time," wrote Theresienstadt and Auschwitz survivor Zdenek Lederer, "it has been the lot of the Jews to deliver to men a warning . . . that violence is in the end self-destructive, power futile, and the human spirit unconquerable."[114]

The Holocaust was the most recent of these warnings. In its aftermath, Lederer's words have proven true. The German people saw their nation destroyed—physically, economically, morally. Much too late, German citizens realized the futility of having followed the demented Pied Piper, Adolf Hitler, on his rise to power. And the world witnessed, in the resilience of the Jewish survivors, that the human spirit could not be conquered or controlled by outside forces. "Hitler is dead—but I am alive," proudly proclaims survivor Cordelia Edvardson. "Simply to survive," writes Holocaust historian Martin Gilbert, "was a victory of the human spirit."[115]

As Holocaust survivors emerged from the physical, mental, and emotional shock of the Final Solution, many were haunted by the question "Why did I survive when my family and friends did not?" Each one answered the question differently, and some could find no answer at all.

Generally survivors shared this thought: that they had survived to bear witness. They had an obligation to tell the world what they had seen and experienced. A message carved in black granite on a wall at the United States Holocaust Memorial Museum reminds them: "*You are my witness*," reads the quotation from the biblical book of Isaiah. If survivors could make people understand the horrors of the Holocaust, they might keep such a tragedy from occurring again.

Living with the Past

Over the years, most survivors found ways to cope with their experiences and their memories and learned how to rebuild their lives. But the Holocaust has left permanent, everlasting scars that can never be erased, that survivors carry with them to their graves. Jack Eisner, in his book *The Survivor*, tells of the memories that weigh upon him daily: "I am never truly alone. Thousands of people are always with me. My head is so crowded with ghosts I sometimes think it will burst. My ears ring with cries from the voices of the dead. My dreams flame with horror. My memories are gray with ash. I am a survivor."[116]

Former project director at the United States Holocaust Memorial Museum, Michael Berenbaum, says survivors carry

the burdens of memory, haunting memories, nonheroic memories of worlds shattered and destroyed, of defeat, and of life in its aftermath. . . . Only remembrance could salvage some meaning from the ashes of Auschwitz. The dead had died merely for the accident of their Jewish ancestry. Their deaths could serve as a warning, but only if the story was told from generation to generation.[117]

For many years after the Holocaust, few people wanted to hear the stories survivors had to tell, even though most needed desperately to talk about their experiences. After six years of war, people were tired of misery, desolation, and sorrow. Americans, especially, wanted to move toward a bright, promising future, not dwell on the past. "It's time to get on with life" was the message they sent to survivors. And so, many victims chose not to talk.

Others stayed silent because they felt that only those who had been there could possibly understand them. They didn't want to burden their families with the horrible details of their past. Helen Lebowitz Goldkind chose not to talk "because I was afraid I will talk about it so much. And to me it was if my kids will hear what I have gone through that Hitler will get to them too and I wanted . . . to save them from that."[118]

Often survivors found it easier to speak about their experiences to a stranger or to a nameless audience than to their own families. Parents wanted to protect their children from the horror. They wanted them to lead normal lives, untainted by their parents' experiences. And yet, Jews considered it critical to teach their children the lessons of the past.

Yael Danieli, a researcher who interviews survivors, was surprised when many of them told her she was the first person to show an interest in their stories. Many spoke bitterly about the reception they received in their new communities. "The one thing I wasn't prepared for," one survivor told her, "was the intense loneliness I felt. . . . I was more miserable in the years immediately after the war—actually miserable—than I ever was in the camps."[119]

Survivors Begin to Speak

As they aged, adult survivors felt an urgency to tell their stories. They knew that once they were gone, there would be no eyewitnesses to tell the horrid story. Having seen that the lessons of the Holocaust did little to stop subsequent genocides in Cambodia, Rwanda, Bosnia, and elsewhere, they felt a responsibility to speak out, in the hope that their testimony would help to stop future mass murder. And so they began to speak

In the uniform she wore for three years as a prisoner at Auschwitz, a woman leads a march to the German embassy in London in 1960 to protest continued anti-Semitism in Europe.

publicly, to write their memoirs, to record their stories in oral interviews and on videotape. In time, they found willing audiences.

Survivor Erwin Baum returned to Auschwitz in 1988. When he was there at age thirteen, there was no way out. "This time," recalls Baum, "I walked in because I wanted to, and on the other side of the gate there was a taxi waiting for me whenever I was ready to leave." He went first to the bunk where he had slept, then to the place where he had been tattooed, then to the bench where he was beaten. To those who say that the Holocaust never happened, Erwin Baum has only a few words: "Tell them I was there. I'm real. It happened."[120]

In a few years, most adult survivors of the Holocaust will be dead. Child survivors, many of them now senior citizens, feel the same urgency as their parents and are speaking out to make their stories known. Paula Burger was seven years old when her family was moved into a Polish ghetto. Her mother was arrested by the Nazis and thrown in prison, where she worked as an interpreter for the Germans. Paula believes that just before her arrest, her mother had a premonition of death. "She kept telling me that I had to take care of my little brother . . . that if something happened to her I should take care of him." The premonition proved true. A few months later, Paula's mother was shot by the Nazis and her body thrown into a mass grave. "Later, during those war years, I remember holding on to [my brother] constantly. I always felt guilty if he wasn't in my sight range."[121]

During the Holocaust years, Hava Salter was six to ten years old. With the help of her older brother, who had become a partisan, she lived in the woods and in an underground bunker in the hills along the border between Poland and Czechoslovakia.

At first, her mother and father lived with her, but within a short time, her mother was captured by the Germans. Just before her father died of starvation and disease, he tried to strangle Hava, so that the little girl wouldn't fall into German hands, but she ran away.

Today, Hava is in her sixties, living in England. She recently recorded her story for the archives at Yad Vashem, the Holocaust Martyrs' and Heroes' Remembrance Authority in Jerusalem. In speaking of her survival Hava says:

> I don't know why but I suppose there is an inner force that drives you. Why my brother died and my parents died and everybody. . . . I survived. I don't know. Only God knows. I do not feel guilty that I survived. It was probably meant but I accepted it like I accepted a lot of other things.[122]

Despite a childhood that lacked a secure and stable home, Hava managed to create a close family in her adult life. "I have three children . . . and three grandchildren. . . . They are a great comfort to me. I have a loving husband. Very generous. He is not Jewish, by the way. . . . But he loves me very much and he loves my family. . . . They love him. Happiness came out in the end."[123]

Bearing the Burden of Guilt

In spite of the horrors they had endured, survivors like Hava were able to rebuild their lives, to find love, happiness, and satisfaction. Many of the perpetrators were not. To this day, the German nation lives under a burden of guilt for the misdeeds of its forefathers more than a half-century ago. In the aftermath of the war, society demanded that not only must the perpetrators be punished,

The Second Generation

One of the highest priorities of the survivors of the *Shoah* was to have children, to raise a family. Subconsciously, say psychologists, they wanted to rebuild the family destroyed in the Nazi camps and ghettos, bring back the child murdered at Auschwitz. Oftentimes, the newborn would be named for a lost relative. "The new child would carry a heavy burden," writes researcher Yael Danieli in *The Journey Back from Hell*. "In him, all the lost, but now renewed, hopes of the parents would be vested and he would be expected to live on behalf of the lost child whose name he carried."

Expectations for these children were very high. Their souls were clean, they had not suffered, they would be able to accomplish all of their parents' crushed dreams. They grew up with a mandate to achieve, to succeed, to defy by their existence Adolf Hitler's Final Solution. Many second-generation children found themselves living in the shadow of their dead relatives, carrying not only their names but their personalities and unfulfilled goals. "There was the unspoken expectation," writes Abram Sachar in *The Redemption of the Unwanted*, "that they were to fashion their lives as if they were memorial candles."

Children of survivors carried the additional burden of their parents' instability, nightmares, and psychoses related to their trauma in Nazi hands. Often this translated into guilt on the child's part, that he or she had not endured what the parents had, and therefore could not comprehend suffering. Many times these children intentionally put themselves in dangerous situations, such as volunteering in a war zone, to prove that they could survive under severe stress.

Today children of survivors are middle-aged. Many are trying to cope with the legacy left to them by their parents' suffering. Second-generation support groups have sprung up around the world, where adult children of survivors can come together and share their experiences. One of the most interesting is a group called One by One, based in Brookline, Massachusetts. One by One brings together children of Jewish survivors and Nazi perpetrators. Their statement of purpose reads:

We are the children of survivors of Nazi atrocities who grew up in the shadow of our parents' suffering and trauma. We wrestle with the burden of our parents' traumatic past and its influence on our lives as we try to heal the wounds of inhumanity that must never be repeated or forgotten. We are also the descendants of the Third Reich whose parents or grandparents were perpetrators or bystanders in one of the most evil chapters of human history. We struggle with an inheritance of denial, guilt and shame, and try to build a new identity based on integrity and responsibility.

the victims must be compensated for their suffering. The German government is still making reparations (payments for wrongs done) to Holocaust survivors. By the end of the twentieth century, Germany will have paid more than $30 billion in Holocaust-related claims.

Yet, both the survivors and the German government recognize that reparations were simply a gesture of good faith. No amount of money could lessen the Jews' suffering and sorrow. And although the money was welcomed by most, some survivors looked upon the reparations with disdain. One of these was Yehiel de-Nuir, a survivor known as *Katzetnik* ("concentration camp inmate") 135633, who became a well-known author and poet. In a verse from "Star Eternal," he writes about his mother and sister, who died in the camps:

A former prisoner weeps after revisiting Buchenwald in 1995. For survivors, the Holocaust remains an unforgettable memory.

Of all mothers in the world mine was the most beautiful.

On her way to the crematorium my mother saw my face. I know it.

Because I too, on my way to the crematorium, saw my mother's face.

Mother, now they want to give me money to make up for you.

I still can't figure out how many German marks a burnt mother comes to. . . .

Before my sister was burned in the crematorium of Auschwitz, they shaved off her hair. Seventeen years the golden locks lengthened on my sister's head. Long locks of gold. Seventeen years . . .

My sister, now they want to give me money for you. But I don't know how many German marks your curls should bring." [124]

The Lessons of the Holocaust

Auschwitz survivor Hugo Gryn has called the Holocaust "the destruction of the world in miniature form. . . . It was a denial of God," he says. "It was a denial of man." [125] Gryn is right. With the exception of the Righteous Gentiles who helped Jews go into hiding or escape to partisan units, most of humankind was in denial during the destruction of the Jews.

Building Success Out of Sorrow

William B. Helmreich, a professor at the City College of New York, spent more than six years interviewing Holocaust survivors who had come to the United States. He wanted to see what lessons they could teach that would help other people cope with tragedy and adversity. In his book *Against All Odds*, he lists ten traits shared by the most successful survivors. These people were:

1. *Flexible*—able to adapt and adjust quickly to new situations.
2. *Assertive*—bold and insistent about expressing a belief or a desire.
3. *Tenacious*—persistent or stubborn about a belief or desire.
4. *Optimistic*—positive in their outlook for the future; reluctance to dwell on the past.
5. *Intelligent*—"street smartness" more than academic achievement.
6. *Courageous*—able to take risks in business and family matters; having the strength to go on after a major life change or tragedy.
7. Able to distance themselves from the horrible events of their past.
8. Able to identify themselves with a group, and to work with other survivors to their mutual benefit.
9. Able to gain strength and self-confidence from what they had endured.
10. Able to find meaning in their lives and concrete reasons for going on.

In addition to these traits, most survivors were ingenious—they were quick to spot a new trend or a new way of doing a job that offered more opportunity than the old. And they were willing to work extremely hard to achieve their goals. One survivor says he worked continuous "25-hour days" and never saw his children awake. Another claims not to have taken a vacation during the first seventeen years he was in the United States. Survivors were used to taking care of themselves completely, so they looked for no assistance, no handouts, no welfare. Neither did they whine or complain that life was not fair or that they deserved better.

But the attribute that perhaps did more for survivors than any other was their love of and enthusiasm for life. They had not allowed their experiences to leave them bitter and negative. Rather, they seemed to appreciate the gift of life much more than nonsurvivors. Talking with Helmreich, Rabbi Shlomo Riskin put it this way:

What makes Jews remarkable is not
    that they believe in God
After Auschwitz, but that they have
    children after Auschwitz.
That they affirm life and the future.

Very few people raised a finger to help. The bystanders—those who chose to remain silent, to look the other way, to ignore the mass murder that was taking place—stand equally guilty in history beside the Nazi perpetrators.

Many people besides Hugo Gryn have raised the question "Where was God during the Holocaust?" God's seeming abandonment of the Jews caused many survivors to question their faith and some to reject the existence of God altogether. Nobel Prize–winning survivor Elie Wiesel was a deeply religious man before the Holocaust, but much of his postwar life was spent questioning the presence of God during the Jews' suffering. In *Legends of Our Time* he writes, "Perhaps some day someone will explain how, on the level of man, Auschwitz was possible; but on the level of God, it will forever remain the most disturbing of mysteries."[126]

One explanation comes from Simon Friedman, an author who wrote in the *Jewish Spectator* magazine that God must allow man to make his own mistakes and to direct his own course. If God decided for man what was right and what was wrong or intervened to save a victim from its persecutor, there would be no challenge or reason for people to be good. Says Friedman:

> God cannot interfere in human suffering. This principle is built into the blueprint of the world. God has to limit His power—or there would be no freedom for man. . . . God would destroy the purpose of creation, if He were to interfere with the divinely ordained evolutionary process.[127]

Another explanation says that the Holocaust was the suffering the Jews had to endure in order to be returned to the promised land. This idea follows a long-held principle in Jewish history: redemption through suffering. Israel was, in effect, the

Two former prisoners of Buchenwald walk past the main gate of the camp. Many survivors revisit the places of their most hellish memories in an attempt to make sense of their experiences.

Jews' reward for the horror they endured at Nazi hands. "The sufferings of Auschwitz were not mere happenings," writes historian Paul Johnson. "They were part of a plan. They confirmed the glory to come." God, says Johnson, "was not merely angry with the Jews. He was also sorrowful. He wept with them. He went with them into the gas chambers as He had gone with them into Exile [thousands of years earlier]. . . . The creation of Israel was the consequence of Jewish sufferings."[128]

The World Must Not Forget

In the years since liberation, the world has begun to realize the importance of the lessons of the Holocaust. The *Shoah* was not merely a happening in twentieth-century history. It was a warning to all humankind that if we do not learn its lessons, we are bound to repeat them.

Adolf Hitler knew very well how easily the lessons of history are forgotten. When warned by some of his aides that the Final Solution might mark him as one of the

Deniers and Revisionists

A 1993 survey by the American Jewish Committee revealed that at least 20 percent of Americans think it is possible that the Holocaust never happened. Hard deniers claim that six million Jews were never killed and that the Holocaust is a hoax. Soft deniers acknowledge that the Jews may have died, but say their deaths were not murder; rather, they were the result of war, disease, and starvation. Revisionists want to change the way the Holocaust is presented in history books to support the deniers' views.

Survivors' testimony is the strongest argument against deniers and revisionists, who gain in numbers, especially among young people, as the Holocaust recedes in history. "I do not argue with ignorant people," responded Auschwitz survivor Helen Waterford, when a revisionist called a radio talk show on which she was a guest. "My memories are part of me, are part of my mind and body. They are with me constantly; no separate time must be set aside to think and reflect."

Hava Salter, a child who lost her brother and parents in the Holocaust, learned over the years to live with her loss and her survival, in all but one way. "When I hear any denial, either on television or speech or reading," she said in an oral history interview at Jerusalem's Yad Vashem,

it wells within me and I feel so cross, real anger. Sometimes [I'm] speechless that people can still [deny the Holocaust] after all the documentation, the films. I mean the Germans were very thorough. They wrote everything down. . . . So we have paper documentation, picture documentation and everything. For people to say what they say . . . I don't know how to describe it. I don't know whether it makes you boil, but it makes me boil.

President Clinton (second from left) and Elie Wiesel (right of president) pause to reflect after the eternal flame is lit at the U.S. Holocaust Museum in Washington, D.C.

world's worst demons, he shrugged off the comment. Think of the 1½ million Armenians who were murdered by the Turks in 1915, he reminded his aides, "and who ever speaks about the Armenians today?"[129]

"Never, ever to forget" is one of the goals of the United States Holocaust Memorial Museum in Washington, D.C.

When President Bill Clinton lit the eternal flame during the museum's dedication in 1993, he reminded people that this was not a memorial "for the dead alone, or for the survivors. Most of all it is for those of us who were not there. . . . We will be forever strengthened by remembrance."[130]

Notes

Introduction: The Handful
Who Survived

1. Helen Waterford, *Commitment to the Dead*. Frederick, CO: Renaissance House Publishers, 1987, p. 157.

Chapter 1: The State of
Survivors at Liberation

2. Lambert and Bow, *The Holocaust* (compact disc), third interview with Congressman Dewey Short on May 18, 1975. Minneapolis: Quanta Press, 1994.

3. Quoted in Michael Berenbaum, *The World Must Know*. Boston: Little, Brown, 1993, p. 183.

4. Quoted in Abram Sachar, *The Redemption of the Unwanted*. New York: St. Martin's Press, 1983, p. 4.

5. Lambert and Bow, *The Holocaust*, interview of May 18, 1975.

6. Sachar, *The Redemption of the Unwanted*, p. 16.

7. Quoted in Leni Yahil, *The Holocaust: The Fate of European Jewry*. New York: Oxford University Press, 1990, p. 526.

8. Quoted in Sachar, *The Redemption of the Unwanted*, p. 22.

9. Quoted in Martin Gilbert, *The Holocaust*. New York: Holt, Rinehart & Winston, 1985, pp. 801–802.

10. Elie Wiesel, *Night*. New York: Bantam Books, 1960, p. 109.

11. Waterford, *Commitment to the Dead*, back cover.

12. Quoted in Berenbaum, *The World Must Know*, p. 190.

13. Quoted in Berenbaum, *The World Must Know*, p. 191.

14. Quoted in Gilbert, *The Holocaust*, p. 787.

15. Quoted in Gilbert, *The Holocaust*, p. 793.

16. Quoted in Yehudit Kleiman and Nina Springer-Aharoni, eds., *The Anguish of Liberation*. Jerusalem: Yad Vashem, 1995, p. 19.

17. Berenbaum, *The World Must Know*, p. 191.

18. Quoted in Martin Gilbert, *Atlas of the Holocaust*. Oxford: Pergamon Press, 1988, p. 238.

19. Quoted in Max Hastings, *Victory in Europe*. Boston: Little, Brown, 1985, pp. 179–80.

20. Quoted in Berenbaum, *The World Must Know*, p. 190.

21. Quoted in Berenbaum, *The World Must Know*, p. 186.

22. Sachar, *The Redemption of the Unwanted*, p. xxi.

23. Gilbert, *The Holocaust*, p. 800.

24. Barbara Rogasky, *Smoke and Ashes*. New York: Holiday House, 1988, p. 160.

25. Quoted in Sachar, *The Redemption of the Unwanted*, p. 28.

26. Quoted in Sachar, *The Redemption of the Unwanted*, p. 42.

27. Quoted in Berenbaum, *The World Must Know*, p. 221.

Chapter 2: The Reawakening

28. Berenbaum, *The World Must Know*, p. 190.

29. Sachar, *The Redemption of the Unwanted*, p. xxiii.

30. Quoted in Hastings, *Victory in Europe*, p. 180.

31. Quoted in Gilbert, *The Holocaust*, p. 792.

32. Sachar, *The Redemption of the Unwanted*, p. xviii.

33. Paul Johnson, *A History of the Jews*. New York: Harper & Row, 1987, p. 512.

34. Quoted in Kleiman and Springer-Aharoni, *The Anguish of Liberation*, p. 41.

35. Quoted in Berenbaum, *The World Must Know*, pp. 215-16.

36. Quoted in Sachar, *The Redemption of the Unwanted*, pp. 170, 171.

37. Quoted in Anton Gill, *The Journey Back from Hell*. New York: William Morrow, 1988, p. 42.

38. Quoted in Gilbert, *Atlas of the Holocaust*, p. 238.

39. Quoted in Gilbert, *Atlas of the Holocaust*, p. 237.

40. Quoted in David A. Adler, *We Remember the Holocaust*. New York: Henry Holt, 1989, p. 98.

41. Holocaust & Rebirth (symposium). Jerusalem: Yad Vashem, 1974, p. 99.

42. Quoted in Gill, *The Journey Back from Hell*, p. 57.

43. Quoted in Berenbaum, *The World Must Know*, p. 208.

Chapter 3: Millions of Displaced Persons

44. Douglas Botting, *The Aftermath: Europe*. Chicago: Time-Life Books, 1983, p. 80.

45. Quoted in Botting, *The Aftermath: Europe*, p. 82.

46. Quoted in Berenbaum, *The World Must Know*, p. 205.

47. Botting, *The Aftermath: Europe*, p. 86.

48. Botting, *The Aftermath: Europe*, p. 90.

49. Quoted in Botting, *The Aftermath: Europe*, p. 90.

50. Quoted in Berenbaum, *The World Must Know*, p. 206.

51. Quoted in Azriel Eisenberg, *Witness to the Holocaust*. New York: The Pilgrim Press, 1981, p. 554.

52. Quoted in Berenbaum, *The World Must Know*, p. 207.

53. Quoted in Berenbaum, *The World Must Know*, p. 206.

54. Quoted in Sachar, *The Redemption of the Unwanted*, p. 162.

55. Quoted in Sachar, *The Redemption of the Unwanted*, p. 159.

56. Quoted in Sachar, *The Redemption of the Unwanted*, p. 165.

57. Quoted in Sachar, *The Redemption of the Unwanted*, pp. 205–206.

58. Quoted in Botting, *The Aftermath: Europe*, p. 92.

59. Quoted in Leonard Dinnerstein, *America and the Survivors of the Holocaust*. New York: Columbia University Press, 1982, p. xvi.

Chapter 4: Heading to America

60. Sachar, *The Redemption of the Unwanted*, p. xx.

61. Quoted in Sachar, *The Redemption of the Unwanted*, p. xx.

62. Quoted in Berenbaum, *The World Must Know*, p. 209.

63. Quoted in Sachar, *The Redemption of the Unwanted*, p. 197.

64. Sachar, *The Redemption of the Unwanted,* p. 204.

65. Quoted in Berenbaum, *The World Must Know,* p. 210.

66. Quoted in Gill, *The Journey Back from Hell,* p. 43.

67. Quoted in Gill, *The Journey Back from Hell,* p. 287.

68. Quoted in Gill, *The Journey Back from Hell,* p. 288.

69. Quoted in Berenbaum, *The World Must Know,* p. 216.

70. Quoted in Elinor J. Brecher, *Schindler's Legacy.* New York: Penguin Books, 1994, p. 174.

71. Quoted in Gill, *The Journey Back from Hell,* p. 300.

72. Quoted in Berenbaum, *The World Must Know,* p. 217.

73. Waterford, *Commitment to the Dead,* p. 126.

74. Quoted in Berenbaum, *The World Must Know,* p. 217.

Chapter 5: To Palestine, the Promised Land

75. Johnson, *A History of the Jews,* p. 517.

76. Quoted in Robert H. Ferrell, ed., *The Twentieth Century: An Almanac.* New York: World Almanac Publishers, 1985, p. 116.

77. Quoted in Sachar, *The Redemption of the Unwanted,* p. 234.

78. Quoted in Sachar, *The Redemption of the Unwanted,* p. 235.

79. Quoted in Sachar, *The Redemption of the Unwanted,* pp. 236-37.

80. Quoted in Sachar, *The Redemption of the Unwanted,* p. 210.

81. Botting, *The Aftermath: Europe,* p. 93.

82. Johnson, *A History of the Jews,* p. 517.

83. Quoted in Eisenberg, *Witness to the Holocaust,* p. 557.

84. Quoted in Botting, *The Aftermath: Europe,* p. 95.

85. Quoted in Botting, *The Aftermath: Europe,* p. 99.

86. Quoted in Eisenberg, *Witness to the Holocaust,* p. 571.

87. Quoted in Sachar, *The Redemption of the Unwanted,* p. 186.

88. Quoted in Botting, *The Aftermath: Europe,* p. 109.

89. Quoted in Sachar, *The Redemption of the Unwanted,* p. 215.

90. Sachar, *The Redemption of the Unwanted,* p. 221.

91. Quoted in Johnson, *A History of the Jews,* p. 532.

92. Quoted in Sachar, *The Redemption of the Unwanted,* p. 224.

93. Quoted in Johnson, *A History of the Jews,* p. 525.

94. Quoted in Gill, *The Journey Back from Hell,* pp. 267, 269.

95. Quoted in Berenbaum, *The World Must Know,* p. 212.

96. Zdenka Novak, Letter to author, October 30, 1996.

97. Johnson, *A History of the Jews,* pp. 519–20.

Chapter 6: The Birth of Israel

98. Quoted in Botting, *The Aftermath: Europe,* p. 123.

99. Botting, *The Aftermath: Europe,* p. 114.

100. Quoted in Sachar, *The Redemption of the Unwanted,* p. 231.

101. Botting, *The Aftermath: Europe,* p. 118.

102. Johnson, *A History of the Jews,* p. 521.

103. Sachar, *The Redemption of the Unwanted,* p. 211.

104. Quoted in Sachar, *The Redemption of the Unwanted*, p. 258.

105. Quoted in Johnson, *A History of the Jews*, p. 527.

106. Sachar, *The Redemption of the Unwanted*, p. xxvi.

107. Sachar, *The Redemption of the Unwanted*, p. 272.

108. Quoted in Sachar, *The Redemption of the Unwanted*, p. 281.

109. Johnson, *A History of the Jews*, p. 527.

110. Sachar, *The Redemption of the Unwanted*, p. 269.

111. Quoted in Sachar, *The Redemption of the Unwanted*, p. 294.

112. Quoted in Ellen Galford, ed., *Library of Nations: Israel*. Amsterdam: Time-Life Books, 1986, p. 103.

113. Sachar, *The Redemption of the Unwanted*, p. xxvi.

Chapter 7: Survivors Rebuild Their Lives

114. Quoted in Gilbert, *The Holocaust*, p. 825.

115. Gilbert, *The Holocaust*, pp. 824, 828.

116. Quoted in Konnilyn Feig, *Hitler's Death Camps*. New York: Holmes & Meier, 1979, p. 420.

117. Quoted in Johnson, *A History of the Jews*, p. 517.

118. Quoted in Berenbaum, *The World Must Know*, pp. 219–220.

119. Quoted in Berenbaum, *The World Must Know*, p. 218.

120. Quoted in Adler, *We Remember the Holocaust*, p. 101.

121. Paula Burger, unpublished manuscript, p. 9.

122. Hava Salter, Transcript of interview done at Yad Vashem, Jerusalem, May 27, 1993, Transcript File #03/7041, p. 54.

123. Salter interview, p. 56.

124. Quoted in Eisenberg, *Witness to the Holocaust*, p. 617.

125. Quoted in Gilbert, *The Holocaust*, p. 826.

126. Quoted in Eisenberg, *Witness to the Holocaust*, p. 633.

127. Quoted in Eisenberg, *Witness to the Holocaust*, p. 635.

128. Johnson, *A History of the Jews*, p. 519.

129. Quoted in Sachar, *The Redemption of the Unwanted*, p. 144.

130. Quoted in Eleanor H. Ayer, *The United States Holocaust Memorial Museum*. New York: Macmillan, 1994, p. 13.

Glossary

Aliyah Bet: Often called simply *"aliyah,"* meaning "going up"—the illegal immigration of Jews to Palestine.

anti-Semitism: A hatred of, or prejudice against Jews.

Ashkenazim: The Yiddish-speaking Jews of Eastern Europe, primarily Poland, Lithuania, Latvia, and the former Czechoslovakia.

bystander: One who stands by idly and does nothing during an incident; in the Holocaust, bystanders were those Gentiles who did nothing to help the Jewish victims of Nazi persecution.

communism: A type of government in which all property and goods are owned by the government and are shared equally by the people.

concentration camps: Prison camps set up by the Nazis to house political enemies or people they considered to be subhuman. Prisoners were worked like slaves and often died of starvation or disease.

death camps: Six centers built in Poland by the Nazis for the sole purpose of killing people. Murders were most often performed with a poisonous gas, and the bodies burned in ovens.

deportation: Shipment of victims to death or concentration camps, usually by train in unheated or cooled cattle cars.

Diaspora: Dispersion or scattering of people in foreign lands; when the *D* is capitalized, it refers to the scattering of the Jewish people outside Palestine, beginning about four thousand years ago.

displaced persons: Commonly called "DPs"—Europeans (both Jews and non-Jews) who were left homeless or stranded at the end of World War II and the Holocaust. The Allies set up temporary camps for the DPs in Germany and Central Europe.

emigrate: To leave a country or region to settle elsewhere.

exodus: A mass departure or emigration.

Final Solution: The Nazis' plan to destroy all European Jews.

genocide: The deliberate extermination of an entire group of people, based upon race, religion, ethnic background, political affiliation, or other common characteristic.

Gentile: A non-Jewish person.

Gestapo: The Nazi secret police who were responsible for rounding up, arresting, and deporting victims to ghettos and concentration or death camps.

ghetto: In Hitler's Europe, the section of a city where Jews were forced to live.

Haganah: Palestinian Jewish organization that helped Jewish refugees flee Europe for the promised land. After the birth of Israel, it became the core of the Israel Defense Forces.

Holocaust: The destruction of life by fire. When spelled with a capital *H* it describes the period from 1933 to 1945 when the Nazis murdered six million Jews and persecuted millions more.

immigrate: To enter a country with the intention of settling there.

Iron Curtain: A symbolic "curtain" along the border between the former East and West Germany that appeared in 1949 and lasted until the late 1980s. Shielded by barbed wire and patrolled by tanks and troops, it marked the dividing line between the communist world of Eastern Europe and Asia, and the free world of Western democratic nations.

jihad: A holy war, waged on behalf of the Islamic religion, seen as a duty by Muslims.

Knesset: The Israeli parliament.

KZ: (Say "katzet") Unofficial abbreviation for the German word *Konzentrationslager*, which means "concentration camp."

liberation: The act of freeing the Nazis' victims from death and concentration camps at the end of World War II.

Nazi: An acronym formed from the German word *Nationalsozialist*, describing National Socialists, the political party made powerful by Adolf Hitler. A Nazi was a member of Hitler's political party.

partisans: Bands of independent fighters who lived in the woods or other remote areas and harassed the German army or the SS in an effort to disrupt their actions.

Passover: Holiday celebrating the Jews' escape from slavery in Egypt during biblical times.

perpetrator: One who is guilty of committing a crime; in the Holocaust, perpetrators were the Germans who willingly participated in the Final Solution.

quota: The share or proportion assigned to one part of a group; in the case of Jewish immigration, that portion of immigrants to a country that the government said could be Jewish.

reparation: Payment for a wrong done to a person or group; regarding the Holocaust, refers to the payments made to survivors by the West German government for the evils committed by the Nazis.

repatriate: To return to the country of one's origin and restore citizenship there.

revisionist: A person who favors changing the presentation of an historical event; regarding the Holocaust, revisionists believe that there was no massive persecution of the Jewish people, that if they died at all in the concentration camps, it was the result of normal wartime hunger, disease, and peril.

She'erit Hapletah: A Hebrew phrase meaning "surviving remnant," referring to the European Jews who survived Hitler's Final Solution.

Shoah: The Hebrew term for the Holocaust.

shtetl: Yiddish word for town or village.

Third Reich: *Reich* means "empire." In German history, the first Reich lasted from 962 until 1806, the second from 1871 to 1918. In the early 1920s, Hitler began using the term "Third Reich" to describe his own empire, which lasted until 1945.

truce: An agreement to maintain peace.

Yiddish: Language of the Ashkenazi Jews of Eastern Europe; combination of German and Hebrew.

Yishuv: Hebrew term for the Jewish residents of Palestine in the years before the establishment of Israel.

Yom Kippur: Day of Atonement (making up for) the sins of the past year. Many Jews observe this holy day by fasting.

Zionism: The plan and movement for building a Jewish homeland in Palestine, which led to the establishment of Israel.

For Further Reading

David Adler, *We Remember the Holocaust.* New York: Henry Holt, 1989. The story of the Holocaust told in the words of those who survived it.

Eleanor H. Ayer, *Parallel Journeys.* New York: Atheneum, 1995. The incredible true story of a Jewish Holocaust survivor who teams up with a former high-ranking member of the Hitler Youth to share the lecture stage for ten years.

———, *The United States Holocaust Memorial Museum: America Keeps the Memory Alive.* New York: Macmillan, 1994. A tour through this Washington, D.C., museum in photos, belongings, and words of the Holocaust victims.

Michael Berenbaum, *The World Must Know.* Boston: Little, Brown, 1993. A history of the Holocaust as told in the artifacts and exhibits at the United States Holocaust Memorial Museum in Washington, D.C.

Douglas Botting, *The Aftermath: Europe.* Chicago: Time-Life Books, 1983. A photo history with text of the postwar years in Europe, including the Nuremberg Trials and the founding of Israel.

Elinor J. Brecher, *Schindler's Legacy.* New York: Penguin Books, 1994. The true stories—both during and after the war—of those Holocaust survivors who owe their lives to Oskar Schindler.

Martin Gilbert, *Atlas of the Holocaust.* Oxford: Pergamon Press, 1988. A collection of 316 detailed black-and-white maps showing every aspect of the Holocaust. Text explains the maps.

Lambert and Bow, *The Holocaust.* Minneapolis: Quanta Press, 1994. A compact disc featuring audio, video, still pictures, newsreel footage, documents, and transcripts of interviews with those who experienced the Holocaust firsthand.

Barbara Rogasky, *Smoke and Ashes.* New York: Holiday House, 1988. An excellent introduction to the Holocaust, from the rise of Adolf Hitler to the liberation of the concentration camps.

Elie Wiesel, *Night.* New York: Bantam Books, 1960. Autobiography of this Nobel Prize–winning survivor's account of his years in Auschwitz and Buchenwald.

Works Consulted

Lucy S. Dawidowicz, *The War Against the Jews.* New York: Bantam, 1975. A complete history of the Holocaust by one of the world's foremost experts on the subject.

Leonard Dinnerstein, *America and the Survivors of the Holocaust.* New York: Columbia University Press, 1982. First-person accounts of survivors who immigrated to the United States and how they established new lives in a foreign land.

Azriel Eisenberg, *Witness to the Holocaust.* New York: The Pilgrim Press, 1981. More than a hundred detailed first-person accounts of Holocaust experiences, by everyone from Adolf Hitler to Elie Wiesel.

Konnilyn Feig, *Hitler's Death Camps.* New York: Holmes & Meier, 1979. A thorough account of all the major death and concentration camps, giving detailed descriptions of each when it was in service and an update on what is there today. A history of each camp is provided, along with first-person accounts from those who were prisoners there.

Robert H. Ferrell, ed., *The Twentieth Century: An Almanac.* New York: World Almanac Publishers, 1985. Reference tool giving a short synopsis of every important date in world history during the twentieth century.

Ellen Galford, ed., *Library of Nations: Israel.* Amsterdam: Time-Life Books, 1986. A thorough account, with many full-color illustrations, of the ancient and modern history of the Jewish state, as well as coverage of the ongoing Arab-Israeli conflict and an account of life in the country today.

Martin Gilbert, *The Holocaust.* New York: Holt, Rinehart & Winston, 1985. A history of the Jews of Europe during the Second World War, by one of the most prominent historians of this period.

Anton Gill, *The Journey Back from Hell.* New York: William Morrow, 1988. An oral history featuring conversations with concentration camp survivors.

Max Hastings, *Victory in Europe.* Boston: Little, Brown, 1985. A complete account, illustrated in color, of the activities from D day (June 6, 1944) to VE-day (May 7, 1945). Includes many eyewitness testimonies of soldiers, nurses, liberators, and so on.

Alfons Heck, *The Burden of Hitler's Legacy.* Frederick, CO: Renaissance House Publishers, 1988. A straightforward, candid account of life in the Hitler Youth by one who was thoroughly immersed in the brainwashing of the Third Reich. Focuses on what it has been like for Germans who were teenagers in the Nazi years to live out their lives in Hitler's shadow.

William B. Helmreich, *Against All Odds.* New York: Simon & Schuster, 1992.

Interviews with more than a hundred Holocaust survivors, with accounts of the successful lives they managed to build in America.

Holocaust & Rebirth (symposium). Jerusalem: Yad Vashem, 1974. A series of lectures on the Holocaust delivered at a conference at Yad Vashem in April 1973.

Paul Johnson, *A History of the Jews*. New York: Harper & Row, 1987. A thorough history of the Jewish people, from the time of the ancient Israelites to the present.

Yehudit Kleiman and Nina Springer-Aharoni, eds., *The Anguish of Liberation*. Jerusalem: Yad Vashem, 1995. Testimonies taken from survivors of their thoughts on liberation day, 1945.

Claude Lanzmann, *Shoah: An Oral History of the Holocaust*. New York: Pantheon Books, 1985. The complete text of the film that featured interviews with dozens of survivors who witnessed some of the most brutal and evil events of the Holocaust.

Zdenka Novak, *When Heaven's Vault Cracked*. Braunton, Devon, Great Britain: Merlin Books, 1995. Autobiography of a Yugoslavian partisan who lost her husband, parents, and sister in the Holocaust and survived to begin a new life in Israel.

———, letter to author, October 30, 1996.

One by One, P.O. Box 1709, Brookline, MA 02146; (617) 424-1540. A brochure published by this organization that features text and photos describing the group's purposes and activities.

Abram Sachar, *The Redemption of the Unwanted*. New York: St. Martin's Press, 1983. An account of the Holocaust from the time of liberation of the concentration camps through the founding of Israel.

Hava Salter, [Interview Transcript #03/7041]. Jerusalem: Yad Vashem, 1993. Interview conducted at Yad Vashem with a Polish/Jewish Holocaust survivor who now resides in England.

Andrew Sanger, *Fodor's Exploring Israel*. New York: Fodor's Travel Publications, 1996. An up-to-date travel guide that presents the country and the people of Israel as they are today.

Helen Waterford, *Commitment to the Dead*. Frederick, CO: Renaissance House Publishers, 1987. Autobiographical account of a German/Jewish survivor of Auschwitz and a Czechoslovakian labor camp who immigrated to the United States and eventually teamed on the lecture circuit with a former high-ranking Hitler Youth leader.

Elie Wiesel, *Legends of Our Time*. New York: Schocken Books, 1968. An account of the deeds and visions of some of the extraordinary people encountered by Wiesel, from an ageless Parisian hobo to Elijah, the mysterious guest at his family's last gathering before deportation.

Leni Yahil, *The Holocaust: The Fate of European Jewry*. New York: Oxford University Press, 1990. Considered in Israel to be the finest, most authoritative history of Hitler's war against the Jews.

Index

Picture Credits

Cover photo: Corbis-Bettmann

American Jewish Archives, courtesy of USHMM Photo Archives, 31

AP/Wide World Photos, 15 (bottom), 27, 37, 50, 52, 69

Archive Photos, 62

Archive Photos/American Stock, 34

Archive Photos/Express News, 74

Francis Robert Arzt, courtesy of USHMM Photo Archives, 21

Marc Block, courtesy of USHMM Photo Archives, 41

Franklin D. Roosevelt Library, 40

Gedenkstaette Bergen-Belsen, courtesy of USHMM Photo Archives, 60

Ghetto Fighters' House, courtesy of USHMM Photo Archives, 28

Hebrew Immigrant Aid Society, courtesy of USHMM Photo Archives, 48

Aviva Kempner, courtesy of USHMM Photo Archives, 45

Alice Lev, courtesy of USHMM Photo Archives, 38, 51

Library of Congress, 43, 54

NARA, courtesy of the Simon Wiesenthal Center Library and Archives, 18 (bottom)

National Archives, 14, 15 (top), 18 (top), 26

National Archives, courtesy of the Simon Wiesenthal Center Library and Archives, 11

National Archives, courtesy of USHMM Photo Archives, 22

Novosti/Corbis-Bettmann, 19

Professor Leopold Pfefferberg-Page, courtesy of USHMM Photo Archives, 29

Reuters/Corbis-Bettmann, 32, 81

Reuters/Arne Dedert/Archive Photos, 77

Reuters/Reinhard Krause/Archive Photos, 79

Reuters/Enrique Shore/Archive Photos, 20

Terezin Memorial Museum, courtesy of USHMM Photo Archives, 16

UPI/Corbis-Bettmann, 30, 45, 56, 58, 63, 64, 66, 67 (both)

About the Author

Eleanor H. Ayer is the author of more than two dozen books for children and young adults, several of which deal with social issues. Among them are *Teen Fatherhood*, *Teen Marriage*, *Teen Suicide*, *Stress*, and *Depression*. She has also written several biographies and books dealing with World War II and the Holocaust.

Mrs. Ayer has a master's degree in literacy journalism from Syracuse University's Newhouse School of Journalism. The mother of two boys, she lives in Frederick, Colorado, where she and her husband operate a small book publishing company.